T0302301

Base of the Pyramid Markets in Latin America

This book focuses on the Base of the Pyramid (BOP) in Latin America and examines the role of the markets in serving low-income populations as consumers, distributors, and entrepreneurs. Deep inequalities, violence, and urbanisation characterise the region. Despite the reduction of poverty observed during the first two decades of the 21st century, Latin America is the most unequal region in the world. Outside active war zones, the region has the highest homicide rate in the world and violence and inequality are deeply intertwined. Markets have a crucial role to play in closing this gap and offering job and income opportunities, especially to unemployed youth, paving the way for safer, more peaceful, and sustainable development.

The book also offers a theoretical reflection on the role that community enterprises who manage common-pool resources can play in serving markets and creating income opportunities for the rural poor.

The book is recommended for managers, policy makers, students, and scholars interested in Base of the Pyramid markets and their potential to lift people out of poverty and to promote a more equal society.

Ximena Rueda Fajardo is Associate Professor at the School of Management at the Universidad de los Andes, Colombia.

Marlen Gabriele Arnold is a Professor in the field of sustainability. Currently, she holds the Chair for Corporate Environmental Management and Sustainability at the Chemnitz University of Technology, Germany.

Judy N. Muthuri is Associate Professor of Corporate Social Responsibility at Nottingham University Business School (NUBS), UK and chairs the Social and Environmental Responsibility Group leading the School's UN Principles for Responsible Management Education network.

Stefan Gold is Professor and Chair of Sustainability Management at the University of Kassel, Germany.

Innovation and Sustainability in Base of the Pyramid Markets

Series Editors:
Marlen Gabriele Arnold, *Chemnitz University of Technology, Germany*
Stefan Gold, *Kassel University, Germany*
Judy N. Muthuri, *University of Nottingham, UK*
Ximena Rueda Fajardo, *Universidad de los Andes, Colombia*

For more information about this series, please visit www.routledge.com/Frugal-Innovation-in-Base-of-the-Pyramid-Markets/book-series/FINNBOP

Base of the Pyramid Markets in Latin America

Innovation and Challenges to
Sustainability

**Edited by Ximena Rueda Fajardo,
Marlen Gabriele Arnold,
Judy N. Muthuri and Stefan Gold**

Routledge
Taylor & Francis Group

LONDON AND NEW YORK

First published 2022
by Routledge
2 Park Square, Milton Park, Abingdon, Oxon OX14 4RN

and by Routledge
605 Third Avenue, New York, NY 10158

Routledge is an imprint of the Taylor & Francis Group, an informa business

British Library Cataloguing-in-Publication Data
A catalogue record for this book is available from the British Library

Library of Congress Cataloging-in-Publication Data
Names: Rueda, Ximena, editor. | Arnold, Marlen Gabriele, editor. | Muthuri, Judy N., editor. | Gold, Stefan, editor.
Title: Base of the pyramid markets in Latin America : innovation and challenges to sustainability / edited by Ximena Rueda Fajardo, Marlen Gabriele Arnold, Judy N. Muthuri, and Stefan Gold.
Description: Milton Park, Abingdon, Oxon ; New York, NY : Routledge, 2021. | Includes bibliographical references and index.
Identifiers: LCCN 2021009882 (print) | LCCN 2021009883 (ebook)
Subjects: LCSH: Rural poor--Latin America--History--21st century. | Latin America--Economic conditions--21st century. | Latin America--Social conditions--21st century. | Income distribution--Latin America--History--21st century.
Classification: LCC HC130.P6 B38 2021 (print) | LCC HC130.P6 (ebook) | DDC 339.4/6098--dc23
LC record available at https://lccn.loc.gov/2021009882
LC ebook record available at https://lccn.loc.gov/2021009883

ISBN: 978-1-138-38912-0 (hbk)
ISBN: 978-1-032-04387-6 (pbk)
ISBN: 978-0-429-42416-8 (ebk)

Typeset in Galliard
by Deanta Global Publishing Services, Chennai, India

Contents

Contributors

Marlen Gabriele Arnold, Professor for Corporate Environmental Management and Sustainability, Chemnitz University of Technology, Germany

Roberto Gutiérrez, Associate Professor, School of Management, Universidad de los Andes, Bogotá, Colombia

Stefan Hergert, Research Assistant, Chemnitz University of Technology, Germany

Iván D. Lobo, PhD candidate, University College, London, UK and Assistant Professor, Universidad de los Andes, Bogotá, Colombia

Adriana Puerto, Research Assistant, School of Management, Universidad de los Andes, Bogotá

Diana Trujillo, Assistant Professor, School of Management, Universidad de los Andes, Bogotá, Colombia

Preface

This Latin American edition is the third in a series discussing the challenges and efforts of BOP markets around the world. An Asian edition highlighted institutional voids that prevent the full integration of BOP populations into markets but also proposed ways in which collaboration with NGOs and other tools could help address those voids to generate growth in the Asian continent. The African edition emphasised the difficulties BOP populations face to reap the benefits of globalisation and value creation. Nevertheless, it stressed opportunities for both large companies and social entrepreneurs to seize the prospects BOP markets offer to lift people out of poverty and to enhance markets. Because of their social embeddedness, the African edition proposed that non-governmental organisations can play a key role in raising awareness and can contribute to private strategies for BOP markets.

This present edition focused on Latin America and the Caribbean stresses the role of two actors who can drive growth and development opportunities for the poor: large multinational corporations and community-based enterprises who manage common-pool resources. The cases featured address the poor as consumers, distributors, and suppliers for local and global value chains. As such, the book offers a varied perspective from which to address and understand the role of BOPs as both target markets but also as agents of sustainable development and prosperity.

Latin America and the Caribbean act as a unit, not only in geographic terms, but also because of a shared history of European colonialism, whose imprint can still be seen in the culture, the institutions, and the economic insertion of the region in the globe. The region offers many opportunities for the development of BOP markets: It has the lowest poverty rates of the Global South; it is the most urbanised continent of the developing world; a large portion of the market share a common language and history that has favored the development of a thriving set of "multi-Latinas" (i.e., large transnational corporations that provide mass consumer goods and services and whose capital is homegrown); and the region has abundant available land to supply global commodity markets. But it also faces great challenges: Latin America has the highest income inequality in the world, large unemployment rates, especially among the youth, and many ethnic communities (indigenous and Afro-descendants) in conditions of social and political exclusion. Under these circumstances, addressing BOP markets becomes a golden opportunity to help the region overcome its main setbacks. Using both a theoretical and practical analysis, this book discusses how these challenges can be and are being addressed and what lessons can be derived from such attempts.

In the first chapter, "Insights in Base of the Pyramid contexts in Latin America & the Caribbean—Interviews with BOP experts," Arnold and Hergert offer a short introduction characterising BOP markets and their evolution in the last decades. It then presents the results of three interviews with private-sector experts in Latin America conducted in 2018. They show that BOP contexts are widespread and diverse in Latin America and the Caribbean but also that there are shared challenges and opportunities and current realities that can be addressed in reaching the BOP.

The second chapter, "Commons-based enterprises: Organisational challenges of entrepreneurial development in the context of the rural commons" by Lobo, offers a conceptual discussion that links the literature on common-pool resources to the literature of BOP markets and that specifically addresses the entrepreneurial potential of rural communities who hold and manage local commons (i.e., forests, fisheries, etc.). The chapter identifies four key challenges these communities face when attempting to produce a livelihood by means of the market: Expansion or scaling up, investment in organisational capacity, institutional innovation, and recombination of capital assets. The chapter also reflects on the political role played by commons enterprises and suggests strategies for helping develop commons-based enterprises. These types of enterprises, driven by the BOP, are particularly relevant in the Latin American context where a significant part of common-pool resources is owned and/or controlled by local communities, especially indigenous and other ethnic communities.

The rest of the book is an analysis of seven case studies from six countries in the region. The third chapter, "Leadership, organisational alignment and partnerships against economic exclusion: What do uncommon success stories have in common?" by Gutiérrez, presents two case studies of multinational corporations addressing the poor as consumers in Colombia. One of the companies provides liquid gas services to peripheral communities, while the other offer tiles and other home improvement materials. Both faced institutional voids and required individual leadership, organisational alignment, and partnerships to overcome the difficulties of economic exclusion.

In the final chapter, "Scaling up Inclusive Distribution Networks (IDNs): Inertias against sustainability," Trujillo and Puerto evaluate five Inclusive Distribution Networks that work with women on delivering products to BOP communities in Latin America. The authors show that business models that began as inclusive, open, and cross-sectoral changed to a pure market logic to achieve economic success in the scale-up phase, highlighting the difficulties private companies face in addressing the dual purpose of profit and inclusion and thus the limited success experienced in tapping into BOP markets.

May 2021

Ximena Rueda, Universidad de los Andes, Colombia
Marlen Gabriele Arnold, Chemnitz University
of Technology, Germany
Stefan Gold, University of Kassel, Germany
Judy N. Muthuri, Nottingham University
Business School, United Kingdom

Part I
BOP markets

1 Insights into Base of the Pyramid contexts in Latin America and the Caribbean

Interviews with BOP experts

Marlen Gabriele Arnold and Stefan Hergert

Short introduction

During the last 20 years there have been huge developments and progress globally in terms of income, health, and wealth resulting in a big shift from income levels 1 ($1/day or below) to levels 2 or 3. In 2040 it is expected that the majority of people earning money at level 4 ($32/day and above) will be so-called "non-westerns" (Rosling et al., 2018). However, today, there are still millions of people living in poverty. There are various differences between countries with higher levels of technology, education, expectation of life, basic services, food, etc., and countries with higher levels of poverty and specific diseases, less education, and limited basic services and expectation of life (Arnold, 2018). They differ in terms of technology, sustainability, business models, innovation, and networks, as well as cooperation in science (Rosca et al., 2016; Webb et al., 2010). While these differences exist, countries can be grouped together in terms of income. Rosling et al. (2018) argue for four levels of income—1 ($1/day), 2 ($2 to $8/ day), 3 ($8 to $32/day), and 4 (more than $32/day)—which affect the way of living enormously. Although they have regional differences (e.g., concerning culture, products, food, etc.), the main goods and services are quite comparable (e.g., household products, furnishing, sanitary articles, etc.).

Likewise, comparing contexts of the Base of the Pyramid (BOP), Webb et al. (2010) recognised that BOP markets depend more on formal or informal market characteristics than on country boundaries; hence, the differences in market characteristics within the BOP should be stressed. Closely linked to poverty, BOP characteristics are: (a) low levels of education, skills, and capabilities, (b) weakly established infrastructure in urban areas, almost none in rural areas, (c) dominance of informal contracts and enforcement, including (d) minor property rights protection (Arnold and Sah, 2020). Currently, there are still massive variances in design processes comparing BOP and engineered markets (Jagtap et al., 2014; Silvestre and Silva Neto, 2014). BOP market innovations regularly do not cause technological breakthroughs driving innovation in engineered markets (Zeschky et al., 2014; Brem and Wolfram, 2014; Soni and Krishnan, 2014). BOP solutions are mainly characterised by unique combinations of existing knowledge and technologies on local scales (Govindarajan and Ramamurti, 2011), and BOP markets consider various market participants.

This chapter presents the results of three interviews with private sector experts in Latin America conducted in 2018. Our interviewed experts show the BOP contexts are widely spread and diverse in Latin America and the Caribbean. Their knowledge and understanding of, as well as experience with, BOP contexts in Latin America and the Caribbean are presented in the following interviews. The interviews give a vivid overview of how different BOP settings can be in Latin America and the Caribbean and what the main challenges and opportunities are that critically reflect BOP 1.0 to BOP 3.0 strategies and current realities.

In BOP research, three main perspectives are discussed. The BOP 1.0 strategies focus on selling to the poor. The main presumption was and is that multinational companies (MNCs) can reduce poverty by offering basic and functional goods and services at low costs to BOP markets. This operates as an effective way to combat poverty and social exclusion and increase the standard of living (Prahalad and Hammond, 2002). Yet, the pure provision of goods and services did not properly mitigate poverty and social exclusion (Papaioannou, 2014). Moreover, those practices and strategies were severely criticised by international aid agencies, non-governmental organisations (NGOs), and scientists (Shivarajan and Srinivasan, 2013), and led to BOP 2.0 strategies: Selling with the poor. This means BOP or low-income consumers need to be involved in value creation processes (Simanis and Hart, 2008). Inclusive approaches aim at participating, involving, and cooperating with diverse market actors along the whole value chain. The main presumption is that the employment of local people improves market success and meets the customers' needs more precisely. In addition, according to the literature, BOP 2.0 markets are based on inclusive value creation and frugal innovation; these are narrowly linked. Frugal innovation is a flexible design and production concept based on reduced costs and complexity. In BOP 2.0 contexts, MNCs, NGOs, and small- and medium-sized companies are central players (Arnold, 2018). Casado Caneque and Hart (2015) go even further and argue for BOP 3.0 stressing a total conceptual shift: "Passing from standalone initiatives to innovation ecosystems, from extended distribution approaches to innovation for the last mile, from NGO engagement to cross-sector partnership networks and from poverty alleviation to sustainable development frameworks."[1] The following interviews were conducted in the summer and autumn of 2018 and provide deep insights into fundamental topics and current developments around BOPs in Latin America and the Caribbean. We present the interviews in detail and provide a few common traits in the discussion brought up by the experts that can be very distinct in the Latin American context. The remaining chapters presented in the book discuss specific cases and offer some theoretical perspectives that can be contrasted with the opinions offered here by experts to gain a full understanding of how companies are addressing BOP markets in this particular part of the globe.

The experts

Jenny Melo is a Colombian researcher and consultant who focuses on the analysis of inclusive and green businesses. She combines an intersectional perspective with an understanding of implications and interactions of social, economic, and environmental dimensions of those market-based initiatives. In her more than 10 years of work, she has developed knowledge management processes for all sizes of companies, developmental organisations, NGOs, and small farmers' organisations in Colombia, Ecuador, Argentina, and Spain. Jenny studied business administration and earned a master's degree in social sciences. Since the fall of 2018 she has been living in the United States, pursuing a PhD in Rural Sociology and Sustainability.

Daniel Buchbinder is the Founder and Director of Alterna, a social innovation platform inspiring change in Central America and beyond. Since Alterna's conception, Daniel has led the launch of two social ventures, which serve rural populations at the BOP, and which bring together over 1,500 local entrepreneurs and SMEs, many of which have a significant social or environmental impact in Central America. He leads an international team of top-level professionals that share his passion to cultivate change from the ground up. During the first three years of Alterna's business cultivation program, entrepreneurs and SMEs have improved the lives of more than 2 million people in Guatemala. Daniel holds a BA in Business Administration (ITAM, Mexico) and two MScs: One in Environmental Technology and Business (Imperial College, UK) and one in Environmental Geography (UNAM, Mexico). Daniel devoted the initial years of his career to the consumer market as a marketing executive at L'Oréal. This experience allowed him to understand the ins and outs of consumer marketing and to design customer-oriented solutions based on a deep understanding of customers. He also spearheaded brand and product management for a wide variety of customers in Latin America and Europe. He has consulted for private and public sectors in areas of tourism, mining, and the consumer market in Mexico, Guatemala, Spain, Germany, and the UK.

In 2013 Daniel's expertise was enlisted by the Ministry of Economics in Guatemala to create the National Policy of Entrepreneurship. Daniel has been invited to participate in forums and events around the world to share his experiences of and views on social enterprise and impact investment. In 2013 he formed part of the Mexican Delegation that attended the G20 Young Entrepreneur Alliance in Moscow, Russia. In the same year, Daniel formed the first chapter in Central America for the Mexican Talent Network, an initiative from the Mexican Bureau of Foreign Affairs. Daniel was selected as an Ashoka Fellow in 2016. He has also been named Senior Skoll Fellow and in 2014 was awarded the Innovation for Sustainability Stephan Schmidheiny prize. Since 2016 Daniel has been Co-Chair of the steering committee for the Mexico and Central American Chapter of the Aspen Network of Development Entrepreneurs (ANDE), and he belongs to a range of boards in companies and social impact organisations. Daniel is deeply moved by the power of enterprise as a means to achieve optimal social and environmental balance. As an avid entrepreneur himself, he greatly enjoys engaging in conversations, planning, and, most importantly, executing the business model that will tackle the next tough challenge.

Laura Villa is a sustainability activist and entrepreneur. She has worked for the public and private sector, as well as for international cooperation organisations on social innovation projects. She currently lives in Medellin and works at the social organisation Comfama. Laura Villa holds a B.A. in Literary Hermeneutic from EAFIT in Colombia, a Master in Politics, Art, History and Literature form the Ludwig-Maximilians University at Munchen and is working towards a PhD in Philosophy at Pontificia Universidad Javeriana in Colombia.

We asked all experts the same questions and asked them to respond to several statements.

Interview with Jenny Melo

What are the main characteristics of BOP markets and contexts in Latin American and the Caribbean, in particular concerning innovation, business model, network, and challenges?

Jenny: In Latin America I see two particular trends. On the one hand, small farmers are trying to connect with big companies as a means to have a more stable connection with markets. And on the other, companies are developing new products and services for the so-called BOP.

I think these two arenas are different and need to be addressed analytically with different approaches. I have [been] paying more time in the first one, involved in some initiatives trying to develop inclusive value chains. And in this case, I think we are still in a very initial phase, because we still have the traditional business models that incorporate small farmers in a traditional place in the value chain. Let's think in big companies trying to source from small farmers: They are offering fair price and guarantee in the buy; however, small farmers are just located in the first step of the value chain, so for them there is not much room to earn more money or to develop some innovation. This is the case for the big companies in soft drink and food sectors. There is no transformation there, in terms of status quo.

But in Latin America there are social entrepreneurs developing new business models in order to change the status quo of the small farmers and to bring other kind of commercial relationship. This is the case, for example, of FRUANDES. It's a social entrepreneurship, and they do the same; they source from small farmers. But they changed the business model and try to be closer to them, being more transparent in terms of price and market. And the asymmetry in the relationship is less than in the case, for example, of *big companies* in Colombia and in Latin America. These examples make evident.

I think that we have different players in this ecosystem and that the approach of each player is different. However, the big actor, of course, are the big companies, in this moment. And it's so traditional, but this is the current trend. From my observation, I consider that BOP markets from the customer's perspective are characterised mainly by financial services; that's the most developed section. Services in education and health exist, but they are small and struggle to scale. The issue with the financial services is that the banks are usually charging high fees for these services, which often turns out badly for the people in the long run.

Which main drivers and barriers do you see in BOP contexts?

Jenny: One barrier is that big companies are averse to take the necessary risks for innovation and change in the business models in BOP markets. The BOP communities are taking the big part of the risks, and this is unfair considering the position of each actor in the social structural and its access to conditions to exert agency. All actors in the field of BOP markets are risk averse. I think in order to answer this question, you need to think in the BOP context through the ecosystem lens and see all the different actors and the intersections between them.

One common barrier is the risk feeling aversion. The risk aversion is more present in big companies, not in the social entrepreneurs or in the customers. I think these two actors are open to explore this kind of risk. But big companies and medium-sized companies need to do a lot of investment and to do a lot of efforts in order to create the possibility conditions for this kind of business.

Creating infrastructure will be too much for some companies, because developing this kind of business requires so many things: Flexibility and money and time, but also empathy, but also design thinking ... It requires a lot, and I think the companies are not fully aware about what it means, because is it not an easy market. It can take 4 to 6 years to reach a point earning some financial return.

A driver is market development. In this sense you can explore new markets, other possibilities. This is interesting because you can create differential business models in which the source from small farmers in fair conditions become a value proposition. With this you can [get] access to other kind[s] of financial resources—for example, *impact investing companies.*

Another driver is the expertise and knowledge on BOP markets. In Colombia, for example, we have been working on BOP for the last 10 years. So, there is a bigger group of people understanding what's happening and what is needed in terms of ecosystem to boost this kind of business models. This is a two-sided thing. It is a good thing now, but can turn into a bad thing. I consider that, in the BOP market, the main unattended issues are the ethical questions, specifically the attention to the asymmetry of the relationship between BOP markets and big companies. This lack of perspective is a barrier for more ethical and more win-win business models here. Because now everybody's doing BOP business or inclusive business, but when you are going to analyse these cases, I'm not sure whether they are really inclusive.

How are BOP value co-creation and cross-sector collaboration characterised?

Jenny: These days you can find big and small organisations working on this topic, and some of them are able to do cross-sector collaboration. For example, we have the World Business Council for Sustainable Development (WBCSD) in all regions in Latin America working in inclusive business. This is like a club for big companies. They are able to speak with financial institutions such as the

Inter-American Development Bank (IDB) and can create cross-sectorial initiatives. They have this sphere of influence. However, there are also other smaller
emerging actors trying to support special projects, for example, MinkaDev in
Colombia and Spain, or Alterna in Guatemala, and others in Mexico, Chile, and
Argentina. These actors are working on these topics in Latin America in different
roles trying to improve and expand knowledge about inclusive business in several
companies. There are others trying to [an] build inclusive business, for example
MinkaDev and Alterna. One issue is that there is only limited financial support for
smaller organisations and inclusive business. Five years ago, we had other financial possibilities, for example from the IDB. They had a particular line of work on
inclusive business. During this time, it was possible to access resources specifically
for inclusive business models. But now, this possibility doesn't exist anymore,
and there is a big need to look for the impact investing actors, which are part of
a growing market in Latin America. They are able to give some resources to the
new ideas in this field but not for big companies.

Concerning the cross-sector collaboration, it's not extended, but it is easier to
see it, for example, between academia and some entrepreneurs or academia and
companies. The policy making—there was this time of talking about inclusive
business and BOP in Colombia. Ten years ago, we had two international events
with Stuart Hart and other big names in this field, but I think now it has become
quieter, and the topic is present but with other terms. Today we are not talking
about BOP markets necessarily; we are talking about impact business and other
names. For example, in Latin America we have Empresas B, our name for B
Corporations. It is like a certification: These companies claim that they want to
be the best for the world, and they have this purpose to make the world a better
place through business. It's full of social entrepreneurs. In Colombia, we have a
lot of these companies—this is a growing trend. They are talking about business
with purpose, and you can find BOP business models or inclusive business there.
There are also other names and other labels that refer to this kind of business
approach to alleviate poverty. So, I think this is an issue—this could be a barrier—
but this is part of the reality. As these new labels are appearing, cross-sector
collaboration can be more difficult, because of the different meanings—inclusive
business versus business with purpose versus sustainability and poverty, etc. There
are plenty of actors working under these different labels. This is a challenge to
improve cross-sector collaboration.

What kind of change do you recognise on BOP markets?

Jenny: I see that there are new actors in the ecosystem. Now we are able to have
different conversations and to ask different questions. Now we open the conversation to talk about the different roles of different actors, because in the past the
central idea is that just big companies have the possibility to develop this kind
of business. This idea is changing, and now we are able to think that other small
or medium-size companies or entrepreneurs are able to play an important role in

the context of inclusive business and BOP markets. I think this is an important change that happened in recent years.

There are also more academics working on this topic, and other actors are developing different publications and documents, for example *Food and Agriculture Organisation of the United Nations* (FAO). They have a lot of documents talking about how you can create an inclusive business model with small farmers—as a real inclusive business model—and there are plenty of documented cases. In the past, if you were looking for cases, you just found the same cases: Walmart and Pepsi, and other[s] from banks, and that's it. But now I think there are more possibilities to find other resources. And finally, we are talking about this field but with different names. Now it's not BOP, and that's it. Now it's BOP and sustainability entrepreneurship, or its purpose business with small farmers, etc. Now we have other names and I think it is important, because it changed the sense of these kind[s] of markets. BOP is a strong word—the image and the metaphor that this word creates is different of the image created when you say inclusive business. If you see this situation from [an]other lens, not business, but more social science lens, you are able to see a change in the discourse about this kind of topic, and I think this is also important.

How would you comment on the following statements?

- *Sustainability is no issue and not a driver in the context of BOP.*
  I disagree. Sustainability is an issue and a driver. In several places of Latin America, we face issues [such] as lack of water, and lack of access to particular services. Because we have sustainability issues like those, we can see the role business can play in the context of a solution. For example, we will be facing water scarcity in a few years. This situation is connected to small farms, and we need, as a society, to guarantee that water is available to produce food for everyone in a healthy way. These challenges are drivers for innovation.
- *The SDGs miss BOP markets.*
  I partially agree, due to SDG 2. Talking about food, this goal is indirectly connected with the small farmers. And relating to other SDGs, for example education and health, it is stressed "we need to improve access to these kinds of services, and we need to connect to the small farmer markets in better conditions" … So, I think the problem is framed within SDGs, but it is not clearly stated that you need to develop BOP business models in order to address the situation. But the need of these markets is included within the SDGs—at least in some goals of the SDGs, but it is not completely explicit.
- *Sustainability is more a "western-driven concept" as a local or "homegrown" concept, and thus not helpful in the BOP context.*
  I partially agree. I think the idea of sustainability announced by the UN, and in the context of this environmental situation, yes, it is a western concept. But in this particular statement I would like to mention two things. First, the concept that was developed by the UN and other organisations

have been broadly promoted. Second, Latin America had a rich history on thinking and practice on how we can live in a more balanced way with the planet—maybe it's not sustainability in the way expressed by [the] UN and Brundtland Commission paper. Here is the thing, in Spanish there are two words, "Sostenibilidad" and "Sustentabilidad," to refer to this topic. In English just one exists. For us, in Spanish, you can translate sustainability with these two words, and both have a different meaning. The first is more the mainstream concept, more UN approach. But the other one is more connected with local thinking about sustainability—is more about well-being and balance with nature, making changes in economic structures, and acting under a justice paradigm. It is Sustentabilidad or well-being. There are a lot of thinkers, a lot about organisations, developing concepts and development tools in order to address this concept in a broader way, going beyond the assumptions implicit in the mainstream notion.

- *BOP markets are mainly about money—social and environmental aspects play a minor role.*
  I think, yes. The best world would be one in which you are able to weigh all three sustainability aspects equally, but reality operates within a "business as usual" perspective. If your business model does not create enough money, your model is dead. Now, there is this lack of sustainability. I don't know if it's about imagination or creativity on the long-term consequences, or if the change in market structures is not ready, but in the big markets in Latin America, the most important thing is profitability. And if you don't have it, it doesn't matter if you have a great concept, it doesn't matter if you have value to the poor and to the ecosystems in several ways. If you are not able to make money in the short-term, the business will die.

- *Offering goods and services, as well as creating value for and with the BOP, do not lead to a mitigation of poverty and social exclusion.*
  No, I think the promise BOP makes is that these business models are a mean[s] to mitigate poverty and alleviate social exclusion. Mitigation of poverty would be a consequence of the BOP business models, because the BOP and inclusive business claims that this is the natural outcome; however, I'm not sure. This is just the promise that fuel[s] these initiatives, and it is a big assumption. I'm not completely sure that in the long run this kind of ethics and this kind of goods and services really improve people's quality [of] life. We need more research; we need more data in order to know if this is true or not.

- *BOP markets are dominated by MNCs—SMEs only play a secondary role.*
  I think it's more a marketing thing. The SMEs are playing a substantial role in the development of BOP markets in Latin America. The multinationals are playing a substantial role, but the role of other actors, e.g., small and other kind of business, are equally important, because they have more flexibility, and they can enter more easily in this kind of logic.

- *Inclusive value creation[2] is mainly a theoretical issue.*
  We have the two situations: It's happening, and also it is not happening. As I said before, you can find a lot of cases and initiatives saying "Oh, I've created

a lot of inclusive value creation, and I'm doing a lot," but sometimes it's not true. Sometimes it is. In some cases, it is part of the narrative to present your company in the market; in other cases, it is a real effort. As I said, we need more research and to know more cases to see if this inclusive value creation is happening as a result of an inclusive business model. On the other side, when a concept is really inclusive and attractive, but is difficult and risky, this concept remains a theoretical issue, because we need other mindsets and other business and institutional arrangements to put inclusive value creation into reality.

- *BOP markets are dominated by frugal innovations.*
  Yes, you can find many examples with this kind of frugal innovation.
- *Institutional voids and mechanisms are a major barrier to uplifting people at the BOP through business.*
  Absolutely. The situations of the institutional frameworks in countries in Latin America are a big issue, because it is more expensive to operate in formal markets, because you don't have this incentive to participate in the formal arena of the market. Sadly, in Latin America, corruption is a major issue. It's a huge issue. There is a lack of democracy, economic development, infrastructure, efficiency, etc. I think we have a lot of institutional voids, from public actors to private ones, and all [of] them are a tremendous barrier for real inclusive business.
- *Culture prevents change on BOP markets?*
  Absolutely. I think it's an important question. In the case of the small farmers, there is the practice of informality. And when you are entering an inclusive business, you need to do certain things and find things to work and sign a contract. Some people do not feel very comfortable with this situation—with this formal environment. Culture needs to be understood very broadly: The culture of the BOP people, the culture of the people in other institutions, supportive inclusive business and BOP, the culture of people in business, because they had this idea about what is the expected profitability that you need to have in order to have a successful business. All these ideas create a kind of culture that maybe is not the best for the provision of the inclusive business.

Interview with Daniel Buchbinder

What are the main characteristics of BOP markets and contexts
in Latin American and the Caribbean, in particular concerning
innovation, business model, network and challenges?

Daniel: My contribution is restricted to Central America, mainly Guatemala and potentially Mexico, so I cannot claim that it can be applied to all of Latin America. I am sure Bolivia, Brazil, Peru, which also have BOP markets, may be structured differently. One of the main characteristics is informality; that's how they operate. So, it's with informality; there is very little formal business being done. It's a kind of extreme. Within a very informal setting, there are only a few transnational companies or really big national companies that are able to tap into the BOP markets. Why? Because those BOP markets tend to be rural or marginal areas, away from distribution centers and distribution channels, so it is more expensive to be there and to operate there. I see only extremes happening there. One is within formality—where people are doing formal businesses and mostly trying but not being able to survive there. Only products from multinational or big companies are able to circulate, because they are the only ones that have the resources to absorb the distribution costs to penetrate to this kind of setting. These are the main two characteristics of the BOP markets that I know. For the population that lives there [rural or marginal areas], I think that another big characteristic is a deep lack of education. And with a deep lack of education, I also tend to find a lack of social capital. So, very little trust and very little networks for people in the BOP. I have to say this with [a] certain degree of ambiguity, because there are of course social groups; there are a lot of churches in Guatemala and in North-Central America. There is a lot of Catholic and Evangelical presence. So, one could claim that they can provide some sort of social capital, because it creates community and also because there is the Mayan community and this kind of sense of belonging. This is true, but from a more productive perspective, there are very little active and effective networks because of the lack of social capital and the poor penetration of education. There are few challenges and very little innovation from the BOP markets, … [and] also the innovation that can occur for or within the BOP markets is somehow also restricted. But that doesn't mean that there is no potential to do interesting things with the right approaches. These approaches need a differentiated perspective, with different models, with varied mindsets … and that requires innovation. But it is restricted right now, because there is very little innovation today that can come out from the BOP. Because now we see it only one way, right? Only the way that can come from the outside and can create some sort of innovative dynamics. But one at least frustrating thing for us is that we don't see a lot of lines where innovation can occur from within the BOP markets. I see little leadership from within the BOP. I see few people prepared to change things from within. Because the ideal kind of setting for us is that the same communities project reimagining themselves and have changes for themselves. But that is what we don't see happening because of all the factors that I just mentioned.

Which main drivers and barriers do you see in BOP contexts?

Daniel: Well, drivers … There is so much to be done. There is so much value to provide. That's important—value to provide to people, because I'm sure that you are very well aware that BOP has for some people this notion "let's sell to the poor" There is BOP 2.0 and 3.0 and who knows how many point zeros. But I think that the true evolution of the BOP markets is before trying to sell to the people. BOP people have to be included, even for producing products, and to have the possibilities to be better off. Not only because they are sold cheaper soap or cheaper appliances, etc. I think the right approach and the sustainable approach to BOP is where the driver is to properly create value and try to make those communities and those places better off. So, that would be the main driver. Now, for the ones that want to invest in that process—public, private, civil agencies— of course there are drivers where they can tap into markets that can generate value for them, but it has to be both ways.

Barriers—at least in the countries that I know—the cultural barriers are huge. We are talking about different languages, different cosmogonies, and different understandings of the world—of their own world. We're talking about, let's say, Mayan communities, Mayan indigenous communities, here. So, many things are different for them: Culturally they see time—they perceive it differently ... effort, energy, satisfaction ... a lot of things that are important for marketing, let's say, regarding satisfaction and the value proposition, and all these things for them might be a little bit different. So, there are important cultural barriers that have to be considered and also some kind of more formal legal barriers; it is about the informality. These markets operate mainly by and through a different set of rules. So, most of the businesses that operate there are not legally and fiscally subscribed for example to the government. So, they don't pay taxes: That's another big issue that I'm sure you will see across BOP markets everywhere in the world. Another huge barrier is the lack of education and education with this social capital issue linked to it.

How are BOP value co-creation and cross-sector collaboration characterised?

Daniel: For me, the co-creation goes beyond the creation of a product or a service for the BOP markets, like when they are included in the creation process. For me, it's a co-creation where, whatever happens, an important part of the people living in the BOP will have a possibility with this new value that is trying to be created or designed or implemented in a specific community. The co-creation is to involve them as also creators of value and not receivers of value, so that they will have the opportunity to have a different type of income, for example, or that they can have a different type of opportunities to be part of the distribution channel, or to learn or to improve skills, or just like to improve their well-being—to implement their well-being in some way. For me that is essential in the co-creation process. Yet, I have not seen too many examples that I've been amazed by about co-creation. I'm talking not about the intentions, because I know a lot of people and organisations that have really nice intentions. I'm talking about things that really worked, that are implemented. So, I don't see many cases. In terms of cross-sector collaboration, there is very little genuine collaboration between sectors. Here, the presence of the public sector is very complicated. The penetration of corruption in the government is so big that it prevents most of the private sector agents from wanting to collaborate with the public sector. We don't see that much happening. It is hard to work with the government here. Some try, but it is hard, because whenever they are not corrupt, they are extremely inefficient. What happens in these types of countries is that if you are a very good professional finishing studying who wants to do well—do well for your own sake and for others—it is very rare. If you studied at a good university and if you have ambition and drive, very few people will go to the government. So that speaks a lot about how a large [part] of the government is composed, and then that says a lot about why no one or very few wants to work with the government. So, it's hard. Collaboration between private and public sectors is very shallow and very specific. Collaboration between NGOs and governments tend to be a little bit weak. Collaboration also between NGOs and private, I think it might be growing, but I have not seen amazing cases. There's a lot to be done there. It's very early stages of cross-sector collaboration here comparing to what I've seen happening in Europe, in other parts of the world, even in Asia.

What kind of change do you recognise on BOP markets?

Daniel: From the social entrepreneur's perspective there are interesting models that are kind of penetrating and serving. They are serving the BOP, offering products that of course are needed, regarding, for example, good products for sanitation, for clean water, or solar energy. So, there are companies that are beginning to thrive—like new social enterprises that are penetrating into the BOP Markets. But they are not covering the part of how people from the communities can earn better revenue, learn more, be better integrated into a wider world beyond their community, that they can have more dignified lives. So, there are exercises that are starting to tap into these markets, but I'm not seeing much of that yet—this co-creation or cross-collaboration—I don't see that in a very structural way. So, I am seeing examples and interesting cases, but anything close to structural, that's what I think should be happening. Probably BOP people were involved in the creation; they were part of the pilot and the design phases and everything. But then, there is the value of course that they live better, but at some point. For the next company that brings the new innovation, who knows if they will be able to pay because their income is very restricted. Very few innovations are necessarily thinking in how to bring them more ways to have more or additional revenue that represent income for the families.

How would you comment on the following statements?

*   *Sustainability is no issue and not a driver in the context of BOP.*
    Conceptually for me it's absolutely false. I mean, I think that sustainability is in the core of what should happen in the BOP—in a concept, but in real life it's not necessarily happening. Now some people have access to clean energy, but that will not necessarily be sustainable as a whole if that energy is not fully independent for them. They don't have a certain degree of independence on a technology that they don't own it, for example. Or a way that that's just another expense for them with the very few incomes that they already have. So, conceptually, of course that sustainability is in the core of

what should happen in the BOP, but that does not necessarily happen in the practice at the moment.

- *The SDGs miss BOP markets.*

No, I think they are fully included—again conceptually. Practically, the respective indicators of the 17 SDGs are fully engaged and fully directed or including the BOP. Practically, it will depend, indicator by indicator, in each of the BOPs, but I think that the aim is clear for those SDGs to consider the BOP.

- *Sustainability is more a "western-driven concept" as a local or "home-grown" concept, and thus, not helpful in the BOP context.*

I think it depends. Because what BOP context are we talking about? Are we talking about the rural, very far away BOP market? Or are we talking about urban, marginal BOP market? I think, sustainability for, let's say, in Central America or in Guatemala, in the Mayan indigenous BOP market, a lot of sustainability concepts are very natural and very organic in the way how people think. This statement depends so much on if it's rural, if it's urban, the country, the part of the country, and how organic or artificial sustainability as the western concept is or not. Because for Mayans, there are many things about respecting the resources and the land in a very unique way—part of them, and another part, ironically, they aren't. Because they do not necessarily focus on it, for example chemical fertilisers and pesticides: They are integrated into the way of life for some of them and right now they do not necessarily see how much harm this brings, but how much increment on crop creation it can provide. So, I think right now those concepts are very, very, very different for community by community. It is very contextually—it will change from context to context.

- *BOP markets are mainly about money—social and environmental aspects play a minor role.*

I think that is what is happening right now as BOP markets. When we're talking about the markets, social and environmental aspects are kind of a little bit let aside of the equation. That's what is happening in most cases I know.

- *Offering goods and services as well as creating value for and with the BOP do not lead to a mitigation of poverty and social exclusion.*

Yes, I think that can be true. The fact that there is a number of goods and services that "create value" for and with the BOP, it's not absolutely direct that those services will lead to the mitigation of poverty and social exclusion. Those products can have unintended consequences that have to be very well understood, addressed, and explored for risk mitigation and for poverty and social exclusion.

- *BOP markets are dominated by MNCs—SMEs only play a secondary role.*

That tends to be true. Because the muscle and the amount of resources that you need to invest to create those distribution channels are huge, and very few small or medium companies can tap into those distribution channels. It does not matter if you go to the furthest town; that can take you 7 hours to get there from the nearest big city or to the nearest city, you will always find Coca-Cola, you will always find Frito-Lay. It's what happens; those are the companies that can get there.

- *Inclusive value creation[3] is mainly a theoretical issue.*
  It tends to be the truth. It's mostly theoretical and that it is kind of applied in certain parts of the process of creation, but that does not mean that the value persists in the long run. So, maybe once the product/value/service has been created then the value does not necessarily remain, even when the product has already been distributed or used.
- *BOP markets are dominated by frugal innovations.*
  I think that tends to be the truth. For example, the multinational that says "well, we discovered the big formula, now we'll have a sachet of shampoo with a very small format, etc."—it is a little bit frugal, right? That's kind of most of the cases that I have seen. But I think, there have been interesting exercises more of the kind of business models that can change that. But I would partially agree with the statement right now. So, it is less about frugal innovations, but mainly about products basically providing the basic functions of a product while downsizing them. In terms of using local resources and inclusion I have seen glimpses and isolated examples that are interesting, but if we're talking about structural cases, I have not seen them yet.
- *Institutional voids and mechanisms are a major barrier to uplifting people at the BOP through business.*
  Institutional—from the public perspective or from governments—definitely, there are huge voids. We're talking about basic things—health and education—that are absolutely missing, and if that is not been fulfilled, nothing will change. Whatever products and services are developed, there are huge gaps in education and health that basically are not there, and with that, the void is there. Financial inclusion is different; if there has been some sort of financial inclusion for BOPs, it has been because of the presence of micro-finance and credit cooperatives. That is much more sophisticated here. But even with that, that does not necessarily mean that things change structurally, because education and health have not changed dramatically, and poverty has not changed dramatically. So, even with financial inclusion—the presence of countless micro-finance institutions—things have not changed structurally.
- *Culture prevents change on BOP markets?*
  More than prevents, I think culture needs to be fully integrated into BOP markets and processes for change. I don't see it as a preventer. If that is the way of framing the statement, I think it's a little bit risky. So, for me it is the other way around: Culture needs to be considered as appreciated in a very deep way when we are talking about change for BOP markets. Someone might say "yes, because people here do not have the culture to be integrated," but that is a very shallow way of claiming that it's because of the ancient cultures that BOP markets do not succeed. It cannot be that alone. And that would be extremely egotistical and shallow. So, for me, the

way of framing the issue should be different. And I understand how some multinational directors would claim that, but that is not the way to look at it, from my perspective. It should be seen as something that can characterise the products, or it should at least be taken into consideration.

Interview with Laura Villa

What are the main characteristics of BOP markets and contexts in Latin American and the Caribbean, in particular concerning innovation, business model, network and challenges?

Laura: I would say that there are three main scenarios:

(1) big companies or medium-sized companies creating markets for BOPs because they are profitable multinationals, and big companies or even medium-sized enterprises are realising that they are wasting time in the sense that they hadn't discovered a market that was always there. Now they are realising they can make money with the BOPs.
(2) new enterprises, new entrepreneurs, big corporations from this B-system[4] who are trying to create new kind of business models for bringing social or sustainable solutions. They create businesses that are directly oriented towards these environmental and social goals. That's more emerging, like each time, I think people are graduating from universities without the perspective of having the traditional job in a company making money for their bosses and not for themselves or at least with a social purpose. So that's really changing a lot and in a context like Latin America you can experience that. You see hundreds of digital nomads coming to live here, or entrepreneurs from other countries or from our country (Colombia) trying to create different kinds of BOP markets or generally environmental and social solutions through business but also making money.
(3) the BOP itself. When poverty is too extreme, but people live in an environment that offers technology and basic education, you find very creative and resourceful people, that make the most out of the resources they (have) access to and create their own business(es) which are themselves BOPs.

Which main drivers and barriers do you see in BOP contexts?

Laura: I think innovation is a very important driver. At least it has been in Colombia and especially in Medellín. In this city, a social and urban transformation is happening where innovation has played a key role, and it has been like the latest fashion in terms of drivers. But, coming out of poverty has always been the main driver, and especially in a context such as the Colombian [one], but you can see it in Mexico too. For example, the most innovative people work actually for criminality, for illegal kind[s] of businesses, and, if you would not judge them for being criminal and only focus your attention on how innovative they are, you would actually see, those are the most innovative businesses in Colombia and they have the tendency of being attractive for the innovative kind of people. So yes, I think that desperation and ambition are features of the need of coming out of poverty as a driver. I mean, if there is no ambition, things will always be the same, but ambition makes a difference; ambition is definitely a driver for BOP. The access to information through [the] internet is also a very important driver. Diversity [in] culture is also a driver for BOP contexts. In addition, I think formal education is starting to be overvalued nowadays, because you can really access information, and if you're smart enough to research on your own and do stuff on your own and you have that discipline, education is there. Most of the successful businessman or businesswoman that I know, they went to school, but they didn't finish their studies; they dropped school in third, fourth semester, and they have a great company nowadays, and they didn't need to finish their schools. So, I think access to information and access to learn, not from universities or formal institutions, but from the information that's out there. I think that those would be three main drivers: Innovation, ambition, and access to technology and to information.

And then the barriers: I think, education is also a barrier, at least basic education. If you cannot read or write, you have the technology, but you cannot access the information. So, a lack in education—at some level—is definitely a barrier. Extreme poverty, like the kind of living where you only have a certain amount of money a day, puts a great pressure on you. The pressure of the $1/day life is a barrier. There is nothing, or there's very little you can do to break that poverty circle. You can be very poor, but if you don't break that $1/day dynamic, you won't be able to access other conditions of living. Another barrier is insecurity and criminality. When you live in contexts and backgrounds, like we do, the space is divided, and there's a gang watching one block, two blocks, three blocks, and nothing comes in and nothing comes out without paying a fee. So, that makes it very expensive. You live in the poorest neighborhood, but ironically your lifestyle is more expensive, because you have to pay to all these gangs, these extra taxes that they have. So, I think that's definitely a barrier. I also think this comes attached to education ... not learning a second language—especially English—is definitely a barrier, especially for entrepreneurs or for service economies. Medellín is a very service-oriented economy, but you rarely find someone who can really speak a second language. That's really like luxury here. Everybody says they do, but then it's like a very basic thing of "yes" and "no" and "good" or "bad," but very basic words. When you need them to express themselves in different levels, they can't. This affects a service economy very badly.

How are BOP value co-creation and cross-sector collaboration characterised?

Laura: Medellín is well known for cross-sector collaboration. There was such an extreme violence in the late 80s, we finally realised if we didn't come together as different sectors, we wouldn't overcome that criminality-gangster period.

So, cross-sector collaboration in Medellín is actually easy to do, and it's one of our main competitive advantages when you compare Medellín with other Colombian and even with other Latin American cities. And we actually have like a south-south cooperation[5] platform in which we teach other cities from the world how to create cross-sector collaboration. But I'm only talking about Medellín. If you ask me about the general panorama in Latin America, I would say it needs to collaborate a lot more, especially involving companies in social and environmental causes, because the sectors are really very much apart, and each one is looking at their own interest, and no one is bringing those interests together. The SDGs are trying to, and that's a great step forward that the United Nations is making. But it hasn't been enough, and the SDGs only started three years ago, so there hasn't been enough time to see the results of such efforts. Good, innovative practices with cross-sector collaboration are happening in Medellín. It's really amazing what has been achieved here. Public institutions work with the biggest companies together. For example, in education you can find an alliance, "Businessmen for education," where they work as volunteers to assist public schools to be sustainable and improve their quality. The private sector in Medellin has invested in public school buildings, a[n] innovation institute only for teachers, a science museum, and many other great initiatives that you can visit, and it's all been paid with private sector money. The biggest innovation hub of the city is private and public at the same time. It's funded by the two different capitals and they also collaborate. There is a pact for the city to become more innovative, and they had the goal of 2% of our city GDP invested in innovation until the year 2020, but it has already been reached. It was reached last year, so they had to increase the goal.

We did a study on the collaboration of the big financial funds with the small entrepreneurs for the Inter-American Development Bank. They wanted to bring a USD 20,000,000 fund to Colombia two years ago and they hired us first for researching the market and the possibilities of bringing such fund to Colombia. And we researched the national market and then the Medellín market, which, as I said, is special and different. But it was very ironical because, although it was a lot of money and a great institution with a very important reputation, here in Colombia there was no interest. And they only could open up that initiative in two countries, in Chile and Paraguay, although they were researching several markets at the same time. The reason why Colombia wasn't ready is because most of the local family offices that normally invest in these big funds are not ready for patient capital. Colombia is not ready for patient capital … unlike the US, unlike Canada, unlike Europe, in many cases, where you are not only waiting for fast profit but also for social impact. In social impact funds you need up to 10 years until you start receiving profits. There are some funds like that in Colombia, for example Bamboo Finance or Ventures or Acumen Fund. Some of the biggest funds worldwide have established [themselves] in Medellín or in Bogotá, but we also have some local impact funds. The second problem with the initiative was the businesses pipeline, because most of the start-ups are not even connected with the funds, and when they are, most of them are too social to care about making enough profit so that is worth it for impact funds to invest. So, you have the two extremes very apart from themselves: the sponsors of the funds don't want to take such large risks, and the entrepreneurs are so social and so environmental that they cannot develop a good business model. There is a gap in the middle that the accelerators and incubators should try to fill. And some of them try, but for some reason it doesn't work that well.

What kind of change do you recognise on BOP markets?

Laura: I think it's changing, and it's changing in a good and in a bad way at the same time. Corporations are learning from entrepreneurs a lot, and they are intra-entrepreneuring and that can be very exciting, but it can be very danger-ous as well. Dangerous in the sense that they will industrialise at some point everything, like they always have. And if they do, they will kill the revolutionary spirit that there is in social entrepreneurship right now. Social entrepreneurship is like the new kind of social revolution. They are trying to change things, so it's the closest thing to social revolution right now. And if enterprises make a business out of that, which they are doing—and they will succeed of course—I don't have a doubt about it; they will kill the spirit as they always do. In the end, it's all about making money and not changing things. Because right now, the spirit is great. When you meet these young entrepreneurs, they really want to change things, and they're giving up a lot of opportunities in their lives like stability and security and income and traditional jobs and traditional families. They're giving that up for making their bet to other kind[s] of businesses, and having the feeling that they are contributing to change, to the change that the world needs. It's very important, and I think it's more than a fashion. Of course, some of them will do it because it's fashionable, or because they think it's going to be the new trend. They're opportunists; they are taking their place in the right moment. But most of them do it because they really believe they can make a change, and they're giving up a lot of personal things to make that dream come true. Eventually, that is going to be eaten up by the system, as everything does. As hippies once upon a time, or rock music, or hip hop, or every other kind of social revolution in the last decades. So, this is the grass-roots revolution. The grassroots revolution is happening right now, all over the world. Never in human history before had been so many grassroots social initiatives. If they would come together, and if they would collaborate, they would really have the impact they're looking forward to have. That's the only missing piece—connecting these grassroots. But what is happening is really a revolution. That's my perspective. I couldn't see it in another way. How long is that revolution going to last, and how successful is that revolution going to be? I don't know, but I definitely recognise a change, a positive change. They are gaining force; they are gaining volunteers; they are increasing the impact of their actions, and they are growing. But at the same time, the traditional capitalist mechanisms still copy that model, and to own that kind of grassroots model is also growing in the big enterprise and most probably, they're going to rule over that too.

How would you comment on the following statements?

- *Sustainability is no issue and not a driver in the context of BOP.*
  It is tricky. You could very easily say "right," but I think it's changing, and I think sustainability is gaining importance. It's going to be more and more important each time. Perhaps there are people who can think they can afford to ignore sustainability nowadays, but the price in a short and medium term is going to be very high. Like the managers that are ignoring sustainability now, I'm sure they're going to pay a price for that. So, I think, it's not entirely true. I think it was true. It's starting to be not, and it's definitely not going to be true in some years.
- *The SDGs miss BOP markets.*
  It's perhaps the other way around. I think it is BOPs that miss the SDGs, because the SDGs definitely are considering the BOP markets. For example, if you take a look at the indicators within SDG #2, SDG #8, SDG #11, SDG #5, and SDG #13, they are definitely not missing the BOP markets. You should perhaps ask the question the other way around: Are BOP markets missing the SDGs? That could be perhaps a positive answer, but not the other way around.
- *Sustainability is more a "western-driven concept" as a local or "home-grown" concept, and thus, not helpful in the BOP context.*
  I have an interesting answer for that: you could say "yes," but when you think about our ancestors, the answer is "no." Because our native populations were and still are very sustainable—I mean, they even have the concept of sustainability, because they live in sustainable ways. If you take a look at the Pachamama "cosmovision" (world view) like traditional indigenous in Ecuador, Bolivia, Colombia, and Peru did, they are all about mother earth—the way in which they grow their food, the way they exploit the woods, the way they use their natural resources—they are very, very conscious. They are environmentally sustainable and green. That happened far before the western-driven concept of sustainability. Thus, you couldn't say it's a western driven concept. It's a thing that grew with native populations. We have a lot of that in our cultures. But of course, we also have the Spanish legacy of destroying everything to "conquer." I think that's the strongest force of our culture nowadays and not the native Pachamama spirit. So, I think, yes, in that sense, environmental destruction and capitalism are western-driven concepts, such as the current sustainability. One is the western remedy for the problem the western culture created. They're like part of the same paradigm, so to say. Is it helpful or not in the BOP context? I would say yes, but you cannot extra price a BOP product for being sustainable. It is not like BOP people don't feel the necessity of caring about sustainability, but more like

they don't have the education or the resources to take care of the environment. They are just thinking about surviving. So, I would say, in those cases this is true, but in the native rural areas this is not true.

- *BOP markets are mainly about money—social and environmental aspects play a minor role.*
  That's true in the first scenario of BOP I told you in the first question—the case of the multinationals and medium-sized companies that are trying to make money with the BOP. But I think this is not the case for the other two scenarios. Some big corporations are truly committed to sustainability, and most of the social entrepreneurs or grassroot[s] movements are really trying to change the world, to be good for the world.

- *Offering goods and services, as well as creating value for and with the BOP, does not lead to a mitigation of poverty and social exclusion.*
  A single initiative cannot mitigate poverty and social exclusion. It would be a very big responsibility if someone is expecting that BOP mitigates poverty and social exclusion. Because you need a lot of different interventions—cultural, educational, economical interventions—to mitigate poverty and social exclusion. A lot of different dimensions that you need to work at the same time to get that goal. That doesn't mean that offering goods and services and creating value with the BOP people don't help to mitigate or to contribute—I think they do contribute to the mitigation of poverty. I don't know if social exclusion, perhaps poverty yes, but not necessarily social exclusion. Because if you're thinking of BOPs as BOPs, you are starting by excluding them socially; you are putting them into a category; you are putting them in a position where they are already excluded from the mainstream market. I don't know if excluded, because you are including them in the market dynamics—but you are putting them in a position where you are judging them as poor, as [the] base of the pyramid—you are already putting a label on them. If you put a label on them, you prejudice them and therefore exclude them. To sum up, they don't lead directly to the mitigation of poverty, but they can contribute to the mitigation of poverty.

- *BOP markets are dominated by MNCs—SMEs only play a secondary role.*
  In the case of multinationals, that's true. Because multinationals have core businesses that were based on other market dynamics—they weren't looking at BOPs when they started, and what made them multinationals is definitely not the BOPs. But for Transmetano, a Colombian enterprise, it has been something different. They are the main distributor of natural gas in the entire country having a monopoly position. They created a new business model line: As they have the database of people of the BOP market that uses domestic natural gas, they also know, who are the ones that always pay [for] the services. They have this culture of paying their bills very punctual and complete, and no matter how poor they are, they will pay for their natural gas. Realising they had a BOP, they started wondering "what can we offer them? We are an electricity and natural gas company, but what else can we offer them?" BOPs couldn't access the financial sector, and they wouldn't

be allowed to have credit with a traditional bank, because they are so poor, and they live in the countryside where there are no banks. So, the company created a financial line ... in which they give credit to these people, because they know they pay back in time. As a natural gas company, they started a line that has nothing to do with their core business but bases in a BOP and not in a secondary role.

In a sustainability context, we know natural gas is methane, and methane is one of the most harmful gases for the environment. It's worse than carbon. So, in a sustainability scenario, we know that's not the best, and besides, it's not a renewable resource. Perhaps, the future of this company is capitalising that BOP database that they have—and working with them financially, not as a bank, but as a company that lends money to BOPs. They opened the line that is going to keep them in the market in the future. They took a great step forward investing in BOPs, because their natural gas market is not going to last forever. But the BOP is probably going to last a very, very long time. They will have poor people to lend money to, because our tendency is to have a society that is more and more unequal. So, the BOP seems to be lasting forever.

- *Inclusive value creation[6] is mainly a theoretical issue.*
  No, I have seen too many innovations to say it's just a theoretical issue. It works! It doesn't work in every case, and it's hard that it works, but when it works, it works. So, it's not theoretical. For example, there is a beautiful company in Chile focusing on BOP. It is called Algramo, and it created a successful business model in the BOP. They sell super-small portions of food (rice, oil, salt, beans) for the people that live in the $1/day dynamic. I've known them for 7 to 8 years and they are creating inclusive value. That's the perfect example of creating inclusive value. There are other cases. I wouldn't say it's the mainstream tendency of the market, of course not. But it happens in practice.

- *BOP markets are dominated by frugal innovations.*
  Well, what's frugal? (laughing) Every innovation is, in the beginning, a frugal innovation, because every innovation starts with an idea, an idea that seems perhaps probable, but crazy at the same time. While you are implementing it, it becomes more sophisticated. I wouldn't say BOP markets are dominated by frugal innovations; it is too extreme. In BOP, there are a lot of grassroots entrepreneurs ... Most of them are not so skilled in business models and have these idealistic purposes. Perhaps in that third scenario you have frugal innovations. I don't think multinationals waste time with frugal innovations when they address the BOPs. I don't think medium-sized companies can afford investing in frugal innovations when they address the BOPs. It is only the case for the third scenario, where the entrepreneur is ready to give up a lot of things because they are idealistic, and they are perhaps not aware of everything they are giving up, because they're too young. But if they are successful, the implementation will force them to stop being frugal and start being sophisticated. That's the thing with innovation, that in the early stages

where you are all about ideas, frugality is allowed. But then in implementation, when you have to make a business model out of it, frugality must be banned. You need things that work, that create relevant social value, and also that make money. If you have a very frugal innovation that's working, it's very easy to copy, and this is a world of competition—this is a world where competitors eat you up in a year. And if the competitor has more money and less morals and ethics—which they do, multinationals tend to be like that— they don't care about the social impacts; they don't care about sustainability like the grassroots do. They come and take the profitable, frugal innovation away from you and industrialise it and do it in a larger scale than you can. The only way to stay in the market is to be more sophisticated. And that's the process: From the frugal innovation that works, just like that, in the early stage and the path of implementation where you try and fail until you come up with a product or a service that is so well thought and that is so unique, engaging, and relevant, that it's very difficult to copy. And that's where you can stay in the market in a medium term, in a long term. If your innovation is too frugal, everybody can copy it, and you won't last very long. So that's why I say, it's only the early stages, then you need to sophisticate your innovation in order to survive the market.

- *Institutional voids and mechanisms are a major barrier to uplifting people at the BOP through business.*
  Yeah, I think institutional voids and mechanisms are definitely a major barrier. But at the same time, someone trying to create a BOP market has this condition as a starting point. The reason why there is a BOP is because there are institutional voids and mechanisms. The reason why you go into BOP markets is because you think you can offer something that can help that institutional void. If you don't have that, you don't have an offer for a BOP market, because that's your starting point. Your starting point is a kind of population that has no access to basic services, or not to all of them, that has no means to create relevant value, that has no education. With all these voids you have to work with; those are BOP markets. Understanding that is the first step of creating a product or a service for a BOP market. Trying to overcome that institutional void through a market solution alone is not possible. But understand that the state is not the only one who can help those kinds of populations; but the market has something to do, and grassroots movements have something to do. I think that's a very, very important perspective. If you think the state and the institutions are the only [ones] responsible for ditching the gap/avoiding/making it up all these voids and all these failures, then you are very wrong, you don't have the right perspective to come into BOP markets. You have to be convinced, there's something you can do when you start a BOP market.
- *Culture prevents change on BOP markets?*
  Culture is a very broad term and has a very broad definition. I would say culture prevents change in the BOP markets, but culture is the one that

also makes the change in the BOP markets. The culture of social exclusion—because culture is like a matryoshka (a culture within a culture within a culture)—the traditional westernised culture of racism, of social exclusion, of poor versus rich, that traditional white supremacy culture, prevents change on BOP markets, definitely. But the culture of diversity, sustainability culture of the 21st century, opens the door for BOP markets because that's the kind of culture that is ready for social integration, and that's the kind of culture that grassroots entrepreneurs belong to, and that's the kind of culture that the SDGs belong to. So, we're talking here about one culture, but there is not a thing like *one* culture. For example, in Colombia, we have houses, and next to the kitchen there's always a little room for the maids. And the maids need to live like ghosts; no one can see them while they're cleaning; although they live in the same house, you cannot see them. They wear their special clothes and they prepare the meal. And when they prepare the meal, they eat in the kitchen, and the family eats in the dining room, and no one shares the table with them. If you try to share the table, it's like a revolution. What I'm trying to say is that there are still a lot of people afraid to eat or share with the Afro, the homosexual, or the poor. Everyone has its own fear, and we don't recognise ourselves as the same. That is why we need a culture of diversity, where we can accept the differences of each other—no matter if socially, economic, racial, gender, or whatever. It's just a difference, but in the end we all are just human.

Summary and conclusion

There is a consensus that large, multinational companies are active in the Base of the Pyramid markets of South America. They mainly develop products and services for BOP markets in order to sell these internally. In some cases, these companies also cooperate with local farmers, improving the farmers' financial situations. The experts agree that multinational companies currently dominate the market. The present innovative power of BOP markets is considered to be still low but growing. With the emergence of numerous (social) entrepreneurs and Certified B Corporations, the innovative power of BOP markets is increasing with regard to new, more sustainable business models and commercial relationships. The financial services sector is considered to be the most developed, but it is characterised by very high fees, disadvantaging innovative strength. In general, the BOP markets of Latin America and the Caribbean are structurally very informal and illustrated by market players with severe educational deficits.

The main driver within the BOP context is unanimously identified as the desire to improve the personal living situation of the people within the BOP markets through their inclusion in value-added processes and associated higher incomes. In addition to innovations and market developments, access to information and knowledge via the Internet is powering the development of BOP markets. Cultural diversity is seen as a driver on the one hand, but as an obstacle on the other. Other significant obstacles curbing [the] development of the BOP markets are the lack of basic education (i.e., reading and writing) of many people, as well as extreme poverty and related crime, corruption, and informality.

There are networks of numerous larger and smaller organisations, initiatives, and companies that are committed to more sustainable business practices. Nevertheless, Latin America and the Caribbean as a whole are still young in terms of cross-sectoral cooperation and in terms of the involvement of companies in social and environmental issues. On the other hand, corruption and inefficiency on the government side prevent private players from wanting to cooperate with the public sector. Collaboration between the private sector, educational institutions, and NGOs is growing, but the urgently needed cooperation between entrepreneurs and the financial sector is lacking, although investment funds appear to be available.

All three experts nevertheless see a positive development within the last few years. Both the discourse about and understanding of the term "Base of the Pyramid" have changed and expanded. There has been an increase in scientific publications, and BOP issues are being addressed. In the corporate context, more and more small companies and entrepreneurs are venturing into the BOP market, which previously seemed to be reserved for large companies. Numerous interesting and sustainable business models are developing with new, innovative ideas and concepts. However, as these are described as still too fragmented and unstructured, there is also a fear that this revolutionary spirit of small entrepreneurs will ultimately be devoured by the traditional capitalist mechanisms of large companies and corporations. For this reason, the cooperation and association of these numerous small players is seen as an important determinant for sustainable success.

Notes

1 https://www.bopglobalnetwork.org/pyramid-3-0.
2 According to the UNDP (2010: 18), inclusive strategies build bridges and imbed poor or BOP people "on the demand side as clients and customers and on the supply side as employees, producers, and business owners at various points along value chains."
3 According to the UNDP (2010: 18), inclusive strategies build bridges and imbed poor or BOP people "on the demand side as clients and customers and on the supply side as employees, producers, and business owners at various points along value chains."
4 Certified B Corporations are a new kind of business that balances purpose and profit. They are legally required to consider the impact of their decisions on their workers, customers, suppliers, community, and the environment. This is a community of leaders, driving a global movement of people using business as a force for good. https://bcorporation.net/.
5 South–south cooperation is a practice that emerged in developing countries in order to cooperate among themselves and learn from their best development practices and innovations.

6 According to the UNDP (2010: 18), inclusive strategies build bridges and imbed poor or BOP people "on the demand side as clients and customers and on the supply side as employees, producers and business owners at various points along value chains."

References

Arnold, M. (2018). Sustainability value creation in frugal contexts to foster sustainable development goals. *Business Strategy and Development*, 1(4), Special Issue: The role of SDGs for progressing sustainability, 265–275, https://doi.org/10.1002/bsd2.36.

Arnold, M., & Sah, S. (2020). Insights in Asian Base of the Pyramid contexts. In Arnold, M. et al. (eds.) *Base of the Pyramid Markets in Asia*. London: Routledge.

Brem, A., & Wolfram, P. (2014). Research and development from the bottom up— introduction of terminologies for new product development in emerging markets. *Journal of Technology Management for Growing Economies*, 3(1), 9.

Fernando Casado, C., & Hart, S.L. (2015). *Base of the Pyramid 3.0: Sustainable Development through Innovation and Entrepreneurship*. London and New York: Routledge.

Govindarajan, V., & Ramamurti, R. (2011). Reverse innovation, emerging markets, and global strategy. *Global Strategy Journal*, 1(3–4), 191–205.

Jagtap, S., Larsson, A., Hiort, V., Olander, E., Warell, A., & Khadilkar, P. (2014). How design process for the Base of the Pyramid differs from that for the Top of the Pyramid. *Design Studies*, 35(5), 527–558.

Papaioannou, T. (2014). How inclusive can innovation and development be in the twenty-first century? *Innovation and Development*, 4(2), 187–202.

Prahalad, C.K., & Hammond, A. (2002). Serving the world's poor, profitably. *Harvard Business Review*, 80(9), 48–59.

Rosca, E., Arnold, M., & Bendul, J. (2016). Business models for sustainable innovation. An empirical analysis of frugal products and services. *Journal of Cleaner Production*, 126, 133–145. https://doi.org/10.1016/j.jclepro.2016.02.050

Rosling, H., Rosling, O., & Rosling Rönnlund, A. (2018). *Factfulness*. London: Spectre.

Shivarajan, S., & Srinivasan, S. (2013). The poor as suppliers of intellectual property: A social network approach to sustainable poverty alleviation. *Business Ethics Quarterly*, 23(3), 381–406.

Silvestre, B.S., & Silva Neto, R. (2014). Capability accumulation, innovation, and diffusion: Lessons from a Base of the Pyramid cluster. *Technovation*, 34, 270–283.

Simanis, E., & Hart, S.L. (2008). *The Base of the Pyramid Protocol: Toward Next Generation BOP Strategy* (second ed.). Ithaca: Center for Sustainable Global Enterprise, Cornell University.

Soni, P., & Krishnan, R.T. (2014). Frugal innovation: Aligning theory, practice, and public policy. *Journal of Indian Business Research*, 6(1), 29–47.

UNDP (2010). *Inclusive Market Development. Brokering Inclusive Business Models*. Retrieved from http://www.undp.org/content/dam/undp/library/corporate/Partnerships/Private%20Sector/Brokering%20Inclusive%20Business%20Models.pdf

Webb, J.W., Kistruck, G.M., Ireland, R.D., & Ketchen, D.J. (2010). The entrepreneurship process in Base of the Pyramid markets: The case of multinational enterprise/nongovernment organization alliances. *Entrepreneurship: Theory and Practice*, 34(3), 555–581.

Zeschky, M.B., Winterhalter, S., & Gassmann, O. (2014). From cost to frugal and reverse innovation: Mapping the field and implications for global competitiveness. *Research-Technology Management*, 57(4), 20–27.

Part II

Roles, cooperation, and structure in BOP markets

2 Commons-based enterprises

Organisational challenges of entrepreneurial development in the context of the rural commons

Iván D. Lobo

Introduction

The question of whether entrepreneurial development can offer a way out of poverty for a vast swathe of disadvantaged populations in the world is not new. It resonates with similar inquiries aimed at exploring the role of business and private enterprise in addressing pressing social needs. This underlying motivation inspired the literature addressing the concept of the Base of the Pyramid (BOP), which provided momentum for a renewed academic interest in the economic lives of the poor (Banerjee & Duflo, 2007; Viswanathan et al., 2010). The first generation of BOP studies, following the publication of C.K. Prahalad's seminal book in 2004, focused on the question of how multinational corporations could help alleviate poverty. The main premise was that the millions who live under the "line of poverty" (itself a contentious measure) represent, due to sheer numbers, an attractive, untapped market. Providing companies could innovate to offer products and services customised to the needs and financial possibilities of the poor, profit opportunities for the former and improved socio-economic conditions for the latter would flourish.

Turning the poor into consumers was a controversial premise. Advocates acknowledged the importance of lowering barriers to access markets as a precondition to alleviating poverty (London & Hart, 2004). Detractors pointed out that expanding consumption without addressing underlying structural imbalances and the inherent power asymmetry between corporations and disadvantaged communities was naive and misguided (Arora & Rommijn, 2012), if not a pretext for the commercial exploitation of those in need (Karnani, 2009). In response to these and other criticisms, the second generation of BOP studies widened its focus from looking at the role of multinationals and consumption to considering a broad spectrum of BOP actors, contexts, initiatives, and impacts (Kolk et al., 2014). The new premise focused on the study of business models that could effectively integrate poor communities into different stages of the value chain where they could co-produce and capture more value (London & Hart, 2011; Márquez et al., 2010).

Subsequent contributions have explored the possibilities of entrepreneurship and innovation at the lower end of global markets (Ahlstrom, 2010). The idea of entrepreneurship as a vehicle for tackling poverty and fostering socio-economic development for those in economic disadvantage has an intrinsic appeal. Entrepreneurship conveys an emancipatory promise at the intersection of the autonomy of self-employment and the transformational potential associated with innovation. However, those promises are often hard to keep, especially in such contexts as that of aggregated disadvantages.

This chapter is focused on one such context—the rural "commons" where two characteristics coalesce. The first one is the existence of *common-pool resources*, a type of non-excludable, rivalrous resource (like forests or fishing grounds), whose management and conservation depend on common property regimes. The second one is the presence of "*subaltern*" *communities*, those that occupy a peripheral space in the dominant structures of the global political economy and that derive their livelihoods from the use and management of said resources. Combined, these two characteristics impose significant challenges for the development of productive enterprises.

The purpose of the chapter is to offer theoretical reflections to answer two questions. First, how can commons-based enterprises be characterised? Second, what particular challenges do actors that engage in the development of these enterprises face? These questions arose as a result of observations from the field that suggest that there are particular attributes of the entrepreneurial initiatives pursued by communities who depend on the rural commons that cannot be entirely captured by existing constructs (e.g., community or social enterprise). Since this chapter is conceptual in nature, it is primarily informed by a selective literature review of key contributions—from various disciplines—in the fields of entrepreneurship and the commons. However, it is also informed by insights derived from the analysis of formal interviews, dialogues, and discussions with relevant actors (e.g., rural communities, academics, government agencies, practitioners, consultants, and officials from multilateral organisations) held as part of two related research projects carried out with communities of peasants and rural Afro-descendants in Colombia during the last five years. Shared among these communities—whose livelihoods depend to a great extent on the use of the commons—is their aspiration to develop or their involvement in developing collective enterprises as a way to improve their socio-economic conditions. Specifically, these data were analysed following the technique of "thematic analysis" (Boyatzis, 1998). This technique allowed for a structured analysis that contributed to clarifying the themes and theoretical insights about local entrepreneurial development in the context of the commons as presented in this chapter.

The chapter makes the case for and proposes a definition of *commons-based enterprise* as a special form of community enterprise whose purpose is to commercialise products or services directly derived from the use of the commons. It also analyses the extent of *resource tenure* (i.e., the system of rights, rules, institutions, and processes that regulate the access and use of resources) and the primary *driver for value generation* as two key elements that affect the development of commons-based enterprises. Based on this analysis, the chapter discusses four key organisational challenges: expansion to wider markets, investment in organisational capacity, institutional innovation, and recombination of capital assets. Although this set does not represent an exhaustive account of all possible challenges, it does highlight particular areas in which efforts can be focused in order to help develop commons-based enterprises. Importantly, the challenges examined here are mainly organisational and the primary focus for the analysis is the improvement of economic conditions. However, since commons enterprises may serve more than just economic purposes (Berkes & Davidson-Hunt, 2009), some reflections about their political role are also presented.

Following this introduction, the rest of the chapter is divided into five sections. The first section provides a brief description of common-pool resources and the importance of their study. In the second section, the potential of entrepreneurship as a vehicle for development is discussed. This section also presents, first, the central ideas, approaches, and discussions in the literature about the concept of community enterprises. Second, the working definition of commons-based enterprises proposed in this chapter. The third section presents two dimensions to analyse the development of commons-based enterprises—tenure rights and drivers for value generation. The fourth section discusses four scenarios that illustrate key organisational challenges faced by these enterprises. In the fifth section, some of the political challenges faced by commons-based enterprises are discussed. The chapter ends with some concluding remarks, guidelines for action and future avenues.

What are the commons and why do they matter?

In an article published in 1968, Gareth Hardin first postulated the so-called "tragedy of the commons." Subject to open access and use, he argued, common-pool resources (or "commons") would inevitably be overused and ultimately depleted. People would have incentives to profit individually from overexploitation of the resource because the costs of exploitation would be shared by all those for whom the resource is available. The "tragedy" followed directly from the nature of common-pool resources. These resources are defined around two essential characteristics: They are *non-excludable*, i.e., no individual can be effectively excluded from using the resource, and they are *rivalrous*, i.e., the use of the resource by one individual reduces the availability of the resource for others (Ostrom et al., 1994). Typical examples of this type of resources include forests, fishing grounds, underwater basins, and irrigation systems. Government regulation or privatisation was regarded as the mechanisms necessary to regulate the use of the commons and so avoid the "tragedy."

The seminal contribution of Elinor Ostrom (1990) upended Hardin's argument and set the foundations for what would become the consolidated academic field (and, some argue, also a community of practice) of the study of the commons. Essentially, Ostrom proposed a solution to the "tragedy" based on the argument of institutional diversity or the capacity of local users to design institutions (i.e., common property regimes) in order to "self-regulate" the use of the commons and avoid resource depletion. The foundational explanatory goal in the literature of the commons thus became the analysis of the effects that collective action, decentralised governance, and local institutional arrangements—as opposed to privatisation or centralised state control—have on the conservation of common-pool resources (Ostrom, 1990; Agrawal, 2008). Crucially, common property regimes establish rules for those entitled to use and appropriate the resource in order for them to monitor access and exclude non-users. Under such regimes, therefore, free open access is no longer possible, which, by definition, averts the "tragedy."[1]

Some thirty years of work from scholars in the field of the commons have produced a significant body of knowledge. Identifying the conditions that contribute positively to sustainable local management of common-pool resources has been one of the field's most prominent achievements. These conditions can be grouped into four broad categories: Characteristics of the resources, the nature of the groups that depend on the resources, attributes of the institutional regimes through which resources are managed, and the nature of relationships between the group and external forces and authorities (Agrawal, 2008; Ostrom, 2009). However, the extent of the correlation between those conditions and the specific impact they have on the sustainability of the resource has remained difficult to assess (Baland & Platteau, 1999; Poteete & Ostrom, 2004; Agrawal, 2008).[2]

Studying the commons is important because the livelihoods of substantial parts of communities around the world depend on the sustainable use and management of common-pool resources. Moreover, knowledge and practice around the commons will likely be increasingly more relevant in the coming decades. Adaptation to climate change depends on the capacity to guarantee the sustainable use of local and global commons that are central to the functioning of key ecosystems. Incentivising the annual investment needed to meet Sustainable Development Goals, some USD 4.5 trillion according to estimates (UNCTAD, 2014 cited in Gnych, Lawry, McLain, Monterroso, & Adhikary, 2020), will demand concerted and sustained collective efforts that involve complex institutional arrangements for the sustainable management of socio-ecological systems. Such arrangements transcend the conventional boundaries between sectors and demand governance structures where decision-making is significantly decentralised (Carlisle & Gruby, 2019). Within those arrangements, the role and needs of local communities gain renewed prominence.

Balancing the relationship between the use of the rural commons as sources of economic prosperity and the conservation of those resources is far from trivial. One of the alternatives at hand is the development of commons-based enterprises as potentially effective vehicles to meet the double goal of expanding income sources and mitigating biodiversity degradation, which can prove to be an elusive outcome (Salafsky et al., 2001). However relevant this alternative seems to be, the literature on the commons has paid only oblique attention to the processes whereby commons regimes translate into specific forms of entrepreneurial activity. Efforts have been primarily focused on the role of institutional entrepreneurs (Battilana et al., 2009; Garud et al., 2007) as contributors to the provision of locally produced pubic goods that are part of wider common property regimes (Ostrom, 2005, 2010). Less attention has been paid to the development of other forms of entrepreneurial activity.

Entrepreneurship as a vehicle for development

The importance of developing entrepreneurial forms to manage the rural commons is better understood within the wider inquiry of entrepreneurship as a vehicle for alleviating extreme poverty, which has sparked the interest of scholars from different disciplines. At least three theoretical perspectives have been identified in the literature. The first one studies entrepreneurship as *remediation* understood as ways to grant immediate access to resources for those who need them most. The second perspective studies entrepreneurship as *reform*, focusing on its possibilities to promote substantive institutional change. The third one studies entrepreneurship as *revolution*, a process that can potentially bring about changes in the foundational assumptions of capitalism (Sutter et al., 2019). Less sanguine views about the prospects of entrepreneurship have called into question the notion of entrepreneurial development itself, its assumptions, and the inherent contradictions of "communal entrepreneurialism" and related constructs (Escobar, 1995; Tedmanson et al., 2015).

In response to this and similar critiques, scholars have explored key theoretical relationships like the one between social capital and entrepreneurship (See Peredo & Chrisman, 2006). Underlying this approach there is the assumption that social capital is arguably the most easily accessible form of capital for economically marginalised communities. It is argued that social capital—as both a form of capital that has intrinsic value (Lin, 1999) and a platform from which valuable resources can be accessed (Anderson & Jack, 2002)—favors local development and entrepreneurial action. Specifically, social capital (i) facilitates the identification of opportunities (Johannisson & Monsted, 1997), (ii) provides support when initiating ventures (Light, 1998) and in other stages of entrepreneurial activity (Casson & Della Giusta, 2007), and (iii) configures an enabling socio-economic network or "organising context" (Johannisson, 1988; Johannisson & Nilsson, 1989).

However, some suggest that social capital alone cannot adequately promote entrepreneurship unless key collective, idiosyncratic attributes are factored in. For instance, Light and Dana (2013) argue that social capital promotes entrepreneurship only when supportive cultural capital is in place. Along these lines, some literature focuses on how the endowment of social capital embedded in a community of ethnic and racial minorities, as well as their cultural traits, affects the development of entrepreneurial activity (Light, 2005; Peredo et al., 2004; Ram & Jones, 1998). Relatedly, scholars have studied how entrepreneurship may be understood as a function of widely held values (Lipset, 2000), differences in prior information about opportunities (Shane, 2000), or cultural perceptions of opportunity (Dana & Anderson, 2007). Importantly, contexts of deprivation must not necessarily be a constraint for entrepreneurs. Baker and Nelson (2005) define entrepreneurial bricolage as entrepreneurs providing innovative services or products that "arise from their ability and willingness to refuse to enact commonly accepted limitations" (p. 354) and allows them to "make something out of nothing."

When communities become entrepreneurial

In the attempt to define conceptual frontiers between different types of entrepreneurship, four key elements have been identified in the literature: (i) Individual characteristics of the entrepreneur, (ii) the sector in which entrepreneurship operates, (iii) the processes and resources that it mobilises, and (iv) its primary mission and outcomes (Dacin et al., 2010). The relative emphasis put on each of these elements allows for a classification of at least four distinct types of entrepreneurship, all of which have been studied extensively: Economic, institutional, cultural, and social. (See Dacin et al., 2010 and Peredo & McLean, 2006 for a detailed description.) The last three capture entrepreneurial activity that transcends the focus on economic outcomes to encompass broader "societal" changes, be them the betterment of a relevant social need or the transformation of social institutions. Another outcome-based distinction in the literature is particularly useful for the purpose of this chapter. According to Schoar (2010), *subsistence* entrepreneurs are those who engage in entrepreneurial activity as a means of providing subsistence income or alternative employment opportunities for entrepreneurs and their closer kin. In contrast, *transformational* entrepreneurs are those whose enterprises grow beyond individual subsistence needs to provide jobs and income for others.

Outcome-based definitions, however, have been criticised for their lack of theoretical specificity. According to Santos (2012), in order to engage coherently with their institutional environment and avoid "identity challenges" (Tripsas, 2009 cited in Santos, 2012), a central strategic decision for organisations is whether to adopt a focus on value creation or value capture.[3] This distinction, he argues, provides a clearer conceptual criterion to differentiate social from commercial entrepreneurship. While the former is focused on value creation, i.e., increases in the aggregate utility of society's members after accounting for the opportunity cost of the resources used, the latter is centered on value capture, i.e., the appropriation by an actor of a portion of the value created after accounting for the cost of mobilised resources (Mizik & Jacobson, 2003 cited in Santos, 2012). From this approach, addressing neglected problems with positive externalities is thus defined as the distinctive domain of social entrepreneurship, and achieving *sustainable solutions* to those problems—as opposed to *sustainable organisational advantages*—is deemed its central approach (Santos, 2012).

In line with the emphasis on the inherently collective and relational nature of entrepreneurship as a socially transformative process (Steyaert, 2007), scholars have explored the role of communities as a socio-economic construct. Substantive attention has been devoted to studying the phenomenon of *community enterprises*. However, there is yet no clear consensus on the conceptual boundaries that define a community enterprise. This is partly due to what appears to be the intrinsically multifaceted nature of this form of enterprise and the similarities it shares with other forms (e.g., social enterprise). While community enterprises exhibit business-like attributes, they are not businesses in a conventional sense. They generate income through trading or service provision, as opposed to philanthropy or subsidies, which sets them apart from other third sector organisations (Tracey, Phillips & Haugh, 2005). And yet, their goals transcend the "bottom line" (i.e., economic value generation) to incorporate a wider arrange of non-economic purposes. Additionally, they vary greatly in how they are owned, governed, and managed.

Beyond these commonalities, however, one key defining attribute of community enterprises—that from which the name itself is derived—is that they are rooted in a *specifically defined* community, and they serve (primarily, if not exclusively) the interests of that community or at least parts of it (Somerville & McElwee, 2011). This is not a trivial characteristic. The role of the community as an essential unit of socio-economic organisation is well documented. Despite the emphasis used in specific definitions (cf. Agrawal & Gibson, 1999; Anderson, 1983; Bell & Newby, 1974; Elias, 1974; McMilland & Chavis, 1986; Somerville, 2011), the community is "a natural focus for economic development in those peripheral areas where global forces do not spontaneously merge to initiate development" (Johannisson, 1990, p. 77). This attribute alone confers communities (and community enterprises more specifically) a particularly central role in the study of development at the local level.

Despite the difficulties in conveying a single, unified definition of community enterprises, at least three general theoretical approaches can be identified in the literature. The first one understands community as the *focus* of entrepreneurial activity and provides a broad definition of community enterprise as any whose benefits are directed to a particular community, regardless of whether enterprise members are themselves part of that community (Borch et al., 2008). From this approach, community and social enterprises are difficult to tell apart (Austin et al., 2006; Borch et al., 2008). The second approach understands community mainly as the *locus* of entrepreneurial activity. From this, community enterprises are thought to emerge from the "social platform" provided by a particular community (Johannisson, 1990). A third approach emphasises *ownership* as the key defining criteria. Community enterprises are those over which a specific community has full ownership (Simão & Berkes, 2010) as well as governance prerogatives to manage and sustain the enterprise over time (Van Meerkerk, Kleinhans & Molenveld, 2018). In this approach community enterprises are characterised by democratic governance structures in which members are allowed to take part (Pearce, 2003 cited in Tracey et al., 2005) and/or are defined as operating within democratically governed communities (Somerville & McElwee, 2011).

In an effort to add clarity to the conceptual territory, Peredo and Chrisman (2006) propose the concept of community-based enterprises (CBE). These enterprises are characterised by at least three elements: They are based on available community skills, have multiple purposes (although social value creation has precedence over economic value), and are dependent on community participation. What sets this concept apart is that it treats the community as *completely endogenous* to the enterprise, changing the focus of entrepreneurial activity from an existing or new organisation to the community itself. Furthermore, Peredo and Chrisman (2006) define CBE as "a community acting corporately as both entrepreneur and enterprise in pursuit of the common good" (p. 315). Where some approaches broadly understand the community as a platform for entrepreneurial activity (Borch et al., 2008; Johannisson, 1990), they see it as the enterprise itself.

Some scholars have a critical appraisal of the inherent novelty of the CBE concept. Based on a more nuanced account of the social foundation (or "social base") of ownership and control from which, they claim, any enterprise should be defined, Somerville and McElwee (2011) argue that CBE is only one special type of community enterprise. Specifically, one in which *all sections* of a particular community are involved rather than specific subgroups and "whose social base (the social structure of the community) lies in the CBE itself" (p. 320). For them, community enterprises encompass a wider range of phenomena and organisational forms and are better explained and defined as social enterprises that (i) involve part or all of the members of the community (of place or practice), which is the enterprise's defining "social base"; (ii) encompass multidimensional strategic goals (i.e., economic, social, and political) that define the extent of value creation; and (iii) clearly focuses the actions of its members towards realising those goals.

This conceptual discussion about the construct of CBE highlights the definitional importance of community boundaries. As previously mentioned, for a community enterprise to exist there must be an identifiable community that predates the creation of the enterprise and provides the "social base" on which it is founded. The extent to which the contours of the community match those of the enterprise, however, opens up space for at least three different types of boundaries, as illustrated in Figure 2.1.

This diagram shows that the enterprise's boundaries can (i) be subsumed within the community, when only a part of it is involved; (ii) include the whole community, as is the case for the concept of CBE proposed by Peredo and Chrisman (2006); or (iii) transcend the boundaries of the community when external actors share property and decision-making prerogatives over the resource and/or the enterprise. Differences among these three types have implications for governance innovation, value creation, and value appropriation, as will be discussed in subsequent sections of this chapter.

A working definition of commons-based enterprises

In light of the ideas presented thus far, it is possible to attempt a working definition of commons-based enterprises. This concept could offer the possibility to bridge certain aspects of the literatures of the commons and entrepreneurship, a relevant task with potentially fruitful theoretical possibilities.[4] Different names

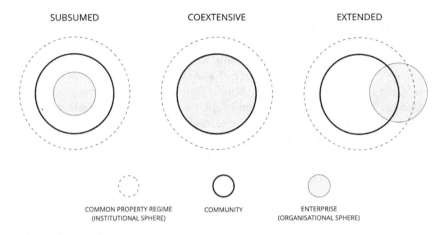

SUBSUMED   COEXTENSIVE   EXTENDED

COMMON PROPERTY REGIME   COMMUNITY   ENTERPRISE
(INSTITUTIONAL SPHERE)   (ORGANISATIONAL SPHERE)

Figure 2.1 Three types of boundaries for community enterprises.

are used in the literature to describe enterprises whose purpose is primarily linked to the use and management of the rural commons. To name but one example, numerous studies use the concept of community forest enterprises (CFEs) as one particular form of community enterprise centered on the commercial use of forest resources.[5] Some define commons-based enterprises as social enterprises (Berkes & Davidson-Hunt, 2009), a characterisation that follows from the emphasis given to social purpose and social innovation as definitional criteria (Ambrose-Oji et al., 2015; Ploman et al., 2017, cited in Gnych et al., 2020).

Any attempt to define commons-based enterprises must therefore include at least two intertwined elements. Following the type of resources mobilised as one of the criteria to conceptualise forms of entrepreneurship, the first of these elements is the *existence of a common-pool resource*. This entails, by definition, the presence of a group of individuals (i.e., a community) with de facto and/or de jure rights to manage and usufruct the resource. From this it follows that the second definitional element is the *centrality of the community*. The theoretical foundations on which the literature of the commons is premised come precisely from the observation that collective governance arrangements—in which the role of the community is prominent, albeit not exclusive—can be at least as effective as other forms of governance to manage resource systems for collective benefit. While there may be discrepancies in the literature of environmental governance, and the commons in particular, about the precise ways to define a community (Agrawal & Gibson, 1999), the centrality of the concept is hardly contested.

Following the ideas presented in the previous section, there are thus theoretical reasons to define commons-based enterprises as a special type of community enterprise, as this chapter does. Building on the definition of community forest enterprises presented by Bray et al. (2005), it is possible to put forth the following working definition: As a special form of community enterprise, a *commons-based enterprise* is any organisational form that, within a common property regime, is set up by a group with a legitimate property right over a common-pool resource in order to commercialise a product or service directly related to the use and/or transformation of said resource. Two key elements in this definition are noteworthy. The first one is that the existence of a common property regime is a necessary condition for the emergence of a commons-based enterprise. In other words, the enterprise—in its organisational form—must be circumscribed by an institution that configures the system of rules on which the management of the common-pool resource is based.[6] The second element is that the definition is flexible in terms of what could be called a double condition of ownership: For a commons-based enterprise to exist, the group or community in question must have at least partial ownership rights over the resource *and* the enterprise set up to commercialise it.

Notably, resource conservation is deliberately left out of the definition. Doing otherwise would impose a normative element on the definition that would turn a contingent outcome into a limiting definitional imperative. In fact, the use and management of the commons implicitly incorporates this outcome.[7] As argued by Berkes and Davidson-Hunt (2009), communities' interest in conserving resources "is not an abstract conservationist ideal" but a recognition that "their survival is linked to the survival of their local environment" (p. 212). It is thus fair to assume that preserving the commons is in the best interest of rational actors whose livelihoods depend on the use of those resources.[8]

Commons-based enterprises: Two analytical dimensions

Different factors affect the capacity of rural communities to set up and organise commercial enterprises. According to Antinori and Bray (2005) those factors include preexisting forms of land tenure, social organisation, experience, and resources. From the specific analysis of community forest enterprises, they also identify four critical sources of tensions: (a) matching hierarchical organisational governance and democratic community governance, (b) "inefficiencies" arising from the interplay between traditional and enterprise structures, (c) corruption and mismanagement, and (d) conflicts over multi-pronged goals. Macqueen et al. (2014) argue that policies to improve natural resource governance and investment in stronger enterprise organisation-building are two critical areas where communities can receive significant support.

Most of these factors (and the tensions they create) can be synthesised in two broad dimensions. The first one, institutional in nature, pertains to the characteristics of the common property regime by which commons-based enterprises are circumscribed and the difficulty of aligning governance structures at the community and organisational levels. Central to the analysis of this dimension there is the extent of *tenure rights* that communities have over common-pool resources. The second dimension is organisational in nature and pertains to predominant orientations and motivations that enterprise members have and the potentially competing demands that come from the pursuit of different types of goals. Central to the analysis of this dimension is the question of the *drivers for value generation* that guides entrepreneurial activity. These dimensions are not only theoretically relevant. They aptly reflect two recurrent considerations that communities and other relevant actors face when considering commons-based enterprises as an alternative for local economic development.

The extent of tenure rights

Property rights, whose importance for economic development has been profusely studied in the literature (Besley & Ghatak, 2010), are at the heart of the study of the commons. A common property regime, or resource tenure, can be defined as "the system of rights, rules, institutions and processes regulating resource access and use" (Cotula & Mayers, 2009, p. 3). Typically, rights over a resource come in the form of devolution from states to communities whereby the latter are granted different degrees of participation in resource tenure.[9] Since common property is not the same as open access, the definition of property rights is as important under common property regimes as it is under strictly private property arrangements.[10]

The importance of resource tenure for the development of commons-based enterprises cannot be emphasised enough. The assertion and management of property rights are at the heart of entrepreneurial development and the design of livelihood strategies (Hindle, 2010). Securing resource tenure gives communities, inter alia, more bargaining power in their relations with governments and businesses (Cotula & Mayers, 2009). Rights, however, are not a universal category. Neither is the degree to which communities participate in resource tenure, which varies greatly across contexts.

Different attempts have been made in the literature to characterise the nature of tenure rights. In their seminal contribution, Schlager and Ostrom (1992) identified a typology comprised of five cumulative "bundles" of property rights over a resource. As summarised by Larson and Dahal (2012), they include:

> Rights to enter the area (access right); to use the land and withdraw resources (use right); to manage the landscape and plan for future use, such as tree planting or timber management (management right); to determine who can and cannot use resources (exclusion right); and to sell or transfer these rights to other parties (alienation right).
>
> (p. 85)

Based on this typology, they make a conceptual distinction between authorised users (those who only have access and withdrawal rights), claimants (those who have access, withdrawal, and management rights), proprietors (those who share the rights of claimants plus exclusion rights), and owners (those who have all five types of rights, including alienation). Scholars have complemented Schlager and Ostrom's typology by integrating it into broader frameworks (Meinzen-Dick & Knox, 2001). Some have added new bundles that better reflect the contemporary complexity of resource tenure where many more social actors are involved and benefits outside of the immediate resource context are considered (Sikor et al., 2017). Others have emphasised the duties that come with tenure rights (cf. Galik & Jagger, 2015).

The literature has also identified regional variations. There are studies that show regional differences in the type and quantity of rights forming a specific resource tenure. When compared to Asia and Africa, Latin America sticks out as one of the regions where the extent of rights devolution seems to be wider. Modalities in this region include community concessions and long-term leases, devolution of rights to user groups, and devolution of collective titles to land and forests (Lawry & McLain, 2012). These characteristics may be explained by the fact that devolution of rights in the region are tied to historic land struggles and institutional reforms aimed at devolving or formally acknowledging the property of indigenous communities over the land they inhabit (Larson & Dahal, 2012).

These and similar contributions highlight the wide variety, complexity, and flexibility in resource tenure as a key analytical insight. Property rights regimes vary widely in terms of how permanent those rights are, how fluid the frontiers defining property over a resource can be, and how much decision-making power communities have to change tenure conditions, among other attributes. No framework can fully capture the breadth and complexity exhibited by property regimes. Critics of Schlager and Ostrom's framework, for example, point out that customary principles of property rights are not actually cumulative but transactional. As argued by Muttenzer (2009), no single rights holder can actually hold the complete set of rights that formally defines state or private ownership.[11] In practice, therefore, actors engage in transactions of incomplete sets of rights.

Notwithstanding the institutional variation inherent in resource tenure and the valid criticisms raised towards neatly defined typologies, for the purpose of the analysis in this chapter it is possible to assume a basic analytical distinction between *limited* and *broad* rights tenure. Following Schlager and Ostrom's distinction, limited tenure includes institutional arrangements where communities are, at most, claimants (i.e., their "bundle" includes access, withdrawal, and management rights over the resource). Broad tenure includes arrangements where communities are either proprietors or full owners. A necessary simplification, this distinction mirrors a similar one identified in many settings between two sets of rights: On the one hand, rights to use and exploit economically the resources over which property rights are exercised, on the other, rights to regulate, supervise, and allocate property (von Benda-Beckmann et al., 2009). Empirically, the distinction is valid as it concurs with the fact that many local communities have been excluded from the democratic decentralisation of resource management and control (Ribot et al., 2006).

One important observation for the analysis presented here is that the existence of tenure rights over a resource system does not by itself solve key issues about the ownership and governance of commons-based enterprises. Communal forms of social organisation provide community members (both individual and organisational) with an institutional "template" for action from which enterprises can flourish. How restrictive or enabling this "template" turns out to be is an important question for understanding the dynamics and evolution of community enterprises in specific domains and contexts. As will be further analysed in the "Four scenarios and key challenges" section, there is not necessarily a direct correspondence between the governance rules of a common property regime and those of a commons-based enterprise.

Drivers for value creation

In an effort to incorporate dimensions that are under-theorised in economic theories of value, scholars have attempted to define other "types" of value (e.g., social and environmental) under the assumption that expanding the concept can better capture theoretical differences between forms of entrepreneurial activity.[12] Strictly speaking, however, all organisations potentially generate a blend of economic, social, and environmental value (Bonini & Emerson, 2005). Differences between types of value are thus a matter of degree more than kind. So, too, should the differences between entrepreneurial forms associated with them be understood.

The pursuit of a wide arrange of goals, as previously mentioned, is one salient characteristic of community enterprises (Peredo & Chrisman, 2006). This means that, in principle, no "type" of value—be it economic, social, or environmental—has intrinsic precedence in determining the main objective to which community enterprises are normatively oriented. However, the working definition of commons-based enterprises advanced in this chapter implicitly emphasises the centrality of economic value creation by incorporating the commercialisation of products or services based on the use of common-pool resources as a central goal. This does not mean that other forms of value are ignored. It does imply, however, that generating sources of income ranks prominently among the priorities of rural communities whose livelihoods depend on some type of communal resource.

As presented in the "Entrepreneurship as a vehicle for development" section, the literature provides a useful theoretical distinction between *subsistence* and *transformational* entrepreneurs. The former engages in entrepreneurial activity as a means to provide subsistence income. The latter do so to create enterprises that grow beyond individual subsistence needs to provide jobs and income for others (Schoar, 2010). Although attempts to categorise entrepreneurial activity based on these two types may be problematic (Rosa et al., 2006), the distinction remains theoretically relevant for it attempts to capture a key underlying motivation driving entrepreneurial activity.

This subsistence/transformational distinction, as originally formulated, is premised on the assumption that certain individual traits of entrepreneurs define their economic objectives, their skills, and ultimately their role in the economy (Schoar, 2010). However, overemphasising character-based explanations for entrepreneurial activity may be misleading. Individual traits and motivations can be more accurately thought of as a function of or, at the very least, mutually dependent on contextual factors. In his "theory of local entrepreneurship in the knowledge economy," Julien (2007) uses the term "entrepreneurial milieu" to refer to both a place and a collective mechanism (i.e., the socio-economic environment surrounding the entrepreneur) that nurtures social ties and provides the resources from which a collective "entrepreneurial spirit" can blossom. From this perspective, individual and collective drivers interact to create enabling conditions for entrepreneurship to flourish. Along similar lines, Macqueen (2013) uses "enterprise-oriented social organisation" to denote a contextual prerequisite for entrepreneurial activity at the community level. This concept evokes a form of collective orientation towards business activity beyond the set of technical skills required for running an enterprise. While those skills may be necessary, they are not sufficient to develop enterprises and entrepreneurial capacity at the community level (Macqueen, 2013).

In light of these considerations, it is possible to argue that the underlying drivers for value creation and entrepreneurial activity in a community reflect both the predominant motivation of certain individuals and/or groups within the community (or even the community as a whole) and the prevailing incentives, resources, and overall predispositions for entrepreneurial activity in their proximate context. Arguably, these factors reinforce each other and are mutually dependent. Borrowing from Schoar's (2010) distinction, for the sake of simplicity, it is possible to categorise those drivers for value generation into two types: *subsistence* and *opportunity*. The former refers to community structures of social organisation where the capabilities for conducting business operations are scarce and the overall set of individual and organisational productive skills is oriented to the satisfaction of subsistence needs in small, proximate markets. Aspirations to expand to wider markets are hardly matched by the set of capabilities available at the community and organisational levels. Conversely, opportunity drivers refer to community structures with effective capabilities for conducting business operations where the overall set of individual and organisational productive skills is oriented to finding and creating opportunities for value creation in proximate and, potentially, wider markets. In this case, the gap between the aspirations to expand to those markets and the set of capabilities available at the community and organisational levels is considerably narrower.

Commons-based enterprises in the global south are often motivated by subsistence needs and built from local economic practices. Customary organisations—Macqueen (2013) rightly contends—are rarely designed for optimally conducting business operations, which is why the entrepreneurial orientation in the social structure of the community is relevant for analytical purposes. Most communities have to learn to "act entrepreneurially." Those that exhibit a distinctive entrepreneurial inclination rooted in community culture, like some reported in the literature, (Peredo & Chrisman, 2006) seem to be exceptional.

Four scenarios and key challenges

When the two dimensions presented in the previous section interact, four possible contexts or scenarios for the development of commons-based enterprises emerge.

PREDOMINANT DRIVER

	Subsistence	Opportunity
Broad Tenure	**Scenario 2** **Organisational Capacity** Resource tenure includes most bundles of rights. Social organisation and capabilities unfavourable for entrepreneurial activities. Collective skills and incentives mostly oriented to satisfying subsistence needs for local groups or markets.	**Scenario 1** **Market Expansion** Resource tenure includes most (if not all) bundles of rights. Social organisation and capabilities conducive for entrepreneurial activities. Collective skills and incentives oriented to pursuing market opportunities.
Limited Tenure	**Scenario 4** **Recombination of capital assets** Communities, as authorised users or claimants, are at most co-managers. Social organisation and capabilities unfavourable for entrepreneurial activities. Collective skills and incentives mostly oriented to satisfying subsistence needs for local groups or markets.	**Scenario 3** **Institutional Innovation** Communities, as authorised users or claimants, are at most co-managers. Social organisation and capabilities conducive for entrepreneurial activities. Collective skills and incentives oriented to pursuing market opportunities.

EXTENT OF RIGHTS

Figure 2.2 Four scenarios in the development of commons-based enterprises.

Figure 2.2 illustrates this interaction and synthesises the characteristics of each of the four scenarios. The name of each scenario highlights the predominant challenge that emerges in each case, which will be explained below.

Scenarios 1 and 2 depict contexts where there is a broad resource tenure that includes most (if not all) of the bundles of rights described by Schlager and Ostrom (1992). In these contexts, groups and communities exercise their role as either full owners or proprietors. The existence of a broad resource tenure provides, in principle, a fair degree of institutional stability derived from the fact that actors (inside and outside the community) can have durable expectations about the conditions under which a resource system is administered. The difference between these scenarios lies in the prevailing driver for value generation. While Scenario 1 illustrates a context where social organisation and collective capabilities are conducive for entrepreneurial activities and skills and incentives are oriented to pursuing market opportunities for value creation, Scenario 2 illustrates those contexts where those capabilities are unfavorable and collective skills are mostly oriented to the satisfaction of subsistence needs. Conditions for the development of commons-based enterprises are more favorable in Scenario 1, where a fair degree of institutional stability meets incentives to pursue market opportunities.

Scenarios 3 and 4, in turn, illustrate contexts where resource tenure is limited, including, at most, co-management rights. In these contexts, groups and communities exercise their role as authorised users or claimants. The limited extent of rights over the resource provides less institutional stability.

The definition of rights may not be entirely clear and thus expectations about the conditions whereby a resource system is administered cannot be reliably sustained. These scenarios are also differentiated in terms of the prevailing driver for value generation. Scenario 3 depicts contexts where the predominant driver is the pursuit of market opportunities. Scenario 4, in contrast, illustrates contexts mainly driven by the satisfaction of subsistence needs for local groups or markets. Conditions for the development of commons-based enterprises are less favorable in Scenario 4, where a limited degree of institutional stability meets a lack of incentives for the pursuit of market opportunities.

Although Scenario 1 depicts, prima facie, the most favorable conditions for developing commons-based enterprises in order to create more value and income opportunities for the community, it is not necessarily a scenario to which every community should aspire. In fact, evidence in the literature shows that certain community enterprises may be more successful when they remain in moderately established markets (Salafsky et al., 2001).

Key emerging challenges

The scenarios that emerge from the schematic representation depicted in Figure 2.2 necessarily simplify what in reality are much more nuanced and "messy" interrelations. Nevertheless, they illustrate the conditions from which at least four central challenges in the development of commons-based enterprises emanate: *identification of and expansion to wider markets, investment in collective organisational capacity, institutional innovation,* and *recombination of capital assets.* It is important to point out that none of these challenges is exclusive to the scenario where they are highlighted. Each challenge becomes particularly relevant in light of the attributes that define each scenario. For instance, the challenge of institutional innovation is relevant across the board, but it acquires preeminence whenever tenure rights need to be expanded in order to facilitate the development of commons-based enterprises.

Identification of and expansion to wider markets

As previously mentioned, Scenario 1 is, in principle, more conducive to the development of commons-based enterprises. A stable rights tenure and an orientation to opportunity drivers, however, are only necessary conditions for enterprise development, which also demands the identification of and expansion to wider markets. This is arguably one of the most difficult challenges for any entrepreneurial initiative that seeks to increase opportunities for value creation. In the context of the commons, this challenge entails additional efforts. Some rural communities are often less equipped with the skills needed to identify market opportunities beyond their immediate sphere of influence. Additionally, balancing out incentives for enterprise growth and resource conservation imperatives is significantly challenging.

The process that leads to the identification of potential market opportunities for the commercial use of a particular common-pool resource is neither straightforward nor linear. In contexts of varied deprivations, the normative trajectory whereby the identification of a market need (and opportunity) precedes the development of an enterprise to address that need is often partially followed at best. Opportunity identification and enterprise creation may be better thought of as an iterative process. Enterprise-oriented forms of social organisation come about through a complex process in which bottom-up motivations of groups or individuals in the community and top-down interventions to make institutional conditions for entrepreneurial activity more favorable gradually reinforce each other.

Importantly, external actors (e.g., NGOs, incubators, governments, cooperation agencies) play a central role in helping communities address the challenge of market identification and expansion. Many commons-based enterprises could hardly embrace market opportunities on their own. The need for sustained support becomes crucial for them. This support entails the participation of third parties who can help communities identify market opportunities most suited to their characteristics and capabilities. Adequately providing this support demands first, "closing the gap between aspirations and capabilities by connecting enterprises to markets so that they can walk the extra mile and create further value," as one consultant with longtime experience in promoting commons-based enterprise development in Colombia and Ecuador put it, and second, distinguishing and balancing out the push of supply and the pull of demand.

Matching the supply capabilities of an enterprise (i.e., what a community can produce or offer) and the potential market demand for a product or service (i.e., what consumers or clients want) is difficult. Particularly so in places where markets are not sufficiently developed, as is the case for many rural communities who are in the process of turning commons into viable entrepreneurial ventures. External actors can thus play a central role in helping communities connect with investors, a critical step in the development of commons-based enterprises (Gnych et al., 2020). Those actors can help communities transit towards "investment readiness," a process whereby managers of commons enterprises gain awareness of and responsive capacity to the needs of potential investors so they can provide financing (Fellnhoffer, 2015 cited in Gnych et al., 2020).

Investment in organisational capacity

In Scenario 2, the predominant challenge for communities is the development of the organisational capacity needed to expand the scope of their entrepreneurial initiatives and, provided it is a desirable goal, transform their predominant driver for value generation so that more value can be created for the community. Since communities in this scenario also enjoy the advantages of a stable rights tenure, their main challenge is strengthening the actual capacity of their organisations to consolidate the foundations of a commercial enterprise.

Investing in organisational capacity—which is often the focus of many initiatives and programs aimed at "community development"—means advancing efforts to either acquire or strengthen specific skills needed for developing an enterprise. These efforts span a wide range from technical and knowledge skills needed to achieve specific objectives to interpersonal skills necessary to work and relate effectively with other actors in the market. Organisational capacity, however, also entails dealing with value-based characteristics that make people more or less receptive to embracing entrepreneurial logics and mindsets. Lowering resistance in order to incorporate certain entrepreneurial worldviews without compromising the shared attributes that give meaning to community membership is an important yet difficult task. Underlying this challenge there is the assumption that "both the attributes defining the community as a whole and an individual's or a group's attitudes and behaviors as a member of the community may influence the kinds of entrepreneurial process that are both feasible and desirable within that community" (Hindle, 2010, p. 612).

As previously stated, the development of enterprise-oriented social organisation may arise from two directions: The work of specific groups, organisations, or federations (at the grassroots level) and/or the initiative of governments. Research shows that both patterns are found in different national contexts (Macqueen, 2013). The emphasis on the investment in organisational capacity is one of the possible theories of change underlying the development of social forms of organisation that are more conducive to the development of commons enterprises. The assumption underlying this particular theory of change is that more capable organisations will eventually help transform the social organisation of the community of which they are part. Given the difficulty in mobilising governments to help create top-down changes, this theory of change is often preferred by actors interested in the development of commons-based enterprises.

The need to strengthen the entrepreneurial capabilities and orientation of the enterprise and the social and institutional context in which it operates is no minor issue. At the heart of this challenge also lies the need to align aspirations and capabilities, as previously mentioned. Lack of clarity in how to develop the skills needed to achieve entrepreneurial aspirations may lead to heightened organisational tensions. Common effects of the misalignment between what the enterprise seeks to achieve and what it is capable of doing include, for example, unrealistic assessments of the characteristics of the market, asymmetrical arrangements to participate in wider value chains, product diversification with no clear knowledge of consumer demand, and oversupply of undifferentiated products.

Institutional innovation

The characteristics of common property regimes vary greatly across regional, national, and local contexts. Finding commonalities across this institutional diversity is arguably one of the prominent goals moving the academic discussion on the commons forward. There are cases—as depicted by Scenario 3—where the social organisation in a community is conducive for entrepreneurial activities and the pursuit of market opportunities, and yet tenure rights are limited. This scenario opens up space for institutional innovation, which entails advancing changes for widening and strengthening the rights tenure regime and/or designing novel governance structures adapted to rights limitations.

Not all communities have the same capacity to instill changes in the institutional settings of which they are part. That includes changes in the common property regime that defines the set of rights for the use of resource systems. Only ideally are communities fully autonomous in the exercise of resource tenure rights. Their decision-making capabilities normally follow from rules at a constitutional level (Agrawal & Ostrom, 2001, cited in Sikor et al., 2017) established by a supra-communal "external authority" (Ostrom, 1999). Widening the bundle of rights is often beyond the control of communities, mostly in contexts where states hold the prerogative of rights devolution (Lawry & McLain, 2012; Macqueen et al., 2014; Monterroso & Barry, 2012; Muttenzer, 2009), external authorities contest local governance institutions (Johnson & Nelson, 2004), and there is limited room for democratic participation from communities.

Changes at the institutional level involve attempts to modify certain characteristics of the common property regime that may have unintended negative consequences for communities. One particular example that the literature analyses is the fact that many common property regimes include provisions that preclude communities from using land as collateral, which compromises their ability to access mainstream financial markets. (For a thorough analysis, see Chapter 9 in Carens, 2000) As argued by Hindle (2010), a common scenario for many indigenous communities who want to engage in the practice of entrepreneurship is that mainstream financial institutions do not grant loans to applicants who operate their businesses on communal property. In these cases, it would be possible, at least in principle, to introduce innovative reforms to facilitate access to credit so that collateral other than land can be used in order to protect communities from exploitation.

Another source of innovation comes from the opportunity to align three nested, institutional "layers" that arguably make up any common property regime: *spatial settings* (a clearly defined territorial boundary), *governance structures*, and *organisational actors*. There are theoretical reasons to expect at least some level of isomorphism between some of these layers. As argued by Peredo and Chrisman (2006), since the structure of a community enterprise is typically rooted in ancestral cultural traditions of community management, it is generally true that the governance structure of a community enterprise "can be expected to be consistent with the structure of decision-making in the community" (p. 320). However, commons enterprises, as organisational actors, may need more organisational flexibility and governance autonomy than the common property regime is able to provide. It may thus be misleading to assume that community enterprises will necessarily mirror the organisational attributes of their community. Even if they do, some enterprises may eventually need to reconfigure some of their structures, rules, and processes to accommodate new demands from their immediate context. Importantly, common property regimes can shape the characteristics of enterprises as much as enterprises can help shape certain attributes of regimes. When it is not a source of critical tensions, this mutual configuration facilitates shared, bidirectional learning and helps enterprises find the optimal fit between their managerial and strategic needs and the characteristics of the common property regime of which they are part.

No serious attempt to answer the question of the promotion and development of commons enterprises can be made without considering the challenge of institutional innovation. Reforms are particularly difficult for they demand the effort and political will of many actors. Particularly important is the role of community associations and other civil society organisations that can advocate for the expansion of tenure rights. Research on forest enterprises shows that grassroots action may be positively associated with the capacity to lobby for better policy environments, among other outcomes associated with effective forest enterprise management (Macqueen, 2013). Notably, the challenge of institutional innovation is particularly suited for institutional or community entrepreneurs (Battilana et al., 2009; McGinnis & Ostrom, 2012) as actors that can have the ability to focus strategic action at the level of both organisations and community (Selsky & Smith, 1994) and help enterprises transition from informal to formal markets (Sutter et al., 2017).

Recombination of "capital assets"

Arguably, the most challenging conditions for the development of commons-based enterprises are those depicted in Scenario 4, which combines limited rights tenure with social organisation and capabilities that are not optimally suited for developing entrepreneurial activities beyond subsistence needs. As argued by Hindle (2010), some communities can be so deprived of the required physical, human, and institutional resources that developing entrepreneurial initiatives becomes unviable. These deprivations characterise what Fraser (1995) calls "bivalent communities," namely those who are simultaneously subjected to economic and cultural discrimination, among other accumulated disadvantages. In these contexts, it is often difficult to talk about entrepreneurship in a conventional sense.[13] However, this does not mean that communities in this particular scenario lack the potential to set up the conditions needed for the development of entrepreneurial activity. Rather, priorities in this scenario shift to enhance the "building blocks" from which productive capacities can develop.

What exactly are those "building blocks"? One way to answer this question is presented in the capitals and capabilities framework. According to this framework, rural communities have at their disposal five types of "capital assets" (i.e., produced, human, natural, social, and cultural capital) that can be combined and transformed in order to expand people's assets bases and design livelihood strategies that respond to their material and experiential needs (Bebbington, 1999). Of these capital assets, social capital is particularly important as it allows communities to access actors and networks that are necessary for them to secure and defend key resources. As mentioned in the "Entrepreneurship as a vehicle for development" section, not only is social capital the most easily accessible form of capital for disadvantaged communities, but it may also be essential for creating economic opportunities in the absence of markets with formal enforcement mechanisms.

However, unlike other forms of capital, social capital is particularly difficult to create exogenously. It means that, when it comes to strengthening social capital, support from third parties is, in principle, much more costly to provide. Consequently, few external actors—if any at all—directly invest in interventions aimed at strengthening social capital as an asset for communities to develop entrepreneurial capabilities. This poses an additional challenge as it prevents key actors from providing the type of support that communities in this scenario mostly need. This barrier is not unsurmountable. Evidence suggests that, in contexts where governments have the capacity and political will to enforce the rights of communities, they are better placed to help communities organise and pressure for the defense of access to resources (Bebbington, 1999).

The political dimensions of commons-based enterprises

Notwithstanding the emphasis made in the definition advanced in this chapter on the economic purpose of commons-based enterprises, they are not only vehicles for creating new income sources. Under certain circumstances, they can also play an important political role. Partly, this role stems from the fact that common property regimes, which are designed to allocate ownership prerogatives among resource users, are naturally incomplete. Often, they are partially defined, strongly contested or sub-optimally enforced. Embedded within those institutional regimes, commons enterprises as organisational actors can compensate for those shortcomings and, eventually, provide a platform to help communities secure access to their resources or strengthen land claims (Berkes & Davidson-Hunt, 2009). This role of commons enterprises is particularly important given that communities are often the weakest party when conflicts over the use of natural resources arise (c.f. Bebbington, 2012; Frapolli et al., 2018; Raftopoulos, 2017).

However, in the process of developing commons enterprises preexisting power asymmetries between communities and other actors can be an onerous barrier to overcome. Moreover, enterprise development inevitably entails expanding the community's socio-economic networks, a process for which *linking social capital* becomes an essential asset. Unlike the horizontal relations inherent to bridging social capital, linking social capital—as defined by Szreter and Woolcock (2004)—entails networks of relationships "between people who are interacting across explicit, formal, or institutionalised power or authority gradients in society" (p. 655). Since not all communities are able to navigate those gradients effectively, it is often hard for them to build and maintain symmetrical power relations with external actors and allies.

The difficulties of overcoming those asymmetries can make some community members distrustful of—if not outright hostile to—the very notion of "entrepreneurial development." In fact, while it is tempting to assume that communities will be equally and unequivocally receptive to the idea of developing commons-based enterprises, the response to local and external forces that emphasise the need to consolidate enterprise-oriented forms of social organisation is not necessarily homogenous or welcoming. As argued by Berkes and Davidson-Hunt (2009), communities respond to those forces with one of two strategies. On one hand, they engage in political resistance that, even if unable to transcend those forces, helps communities adapt them to their particular needs and characteristics, enacting "hybrid" forms of local economic development. On the other, communities develop what Escobar (1995, cited in Berkes & Davidson-Hunt, 2009) calls "transformative engagement" with modernity, or the ability to use business enterprises as a vehicle for development, control of local resources and self-determination. In this case, traditional practices are enriched by "outside" technologies, which in turn may result in adjustments of local socio-economic structures.

Another political challenge for commons enterprises is not derived from the difficulty of dealing with the power asymmetries between communities and external actors but from intra-organisational power struggles. One that is particularly relevant derives from the theoretical distinction made in the literature between value creation and vale capture. As presented in the "Entrepreneurship as a vehicle for development" section organisations must choose between those two orientations in order to define a strategically coherent identity (Santos, 2012). Commons-based enterprises—as conceptualised in this chapter—are of course no exception. In fact, the question of what value the enterprise creates and who can appropriate it may be particularly difficult to answer in cases where the boundaries of the enterprise are subsumed within or extend beyond the boundaries of the community, as shown in the typology presented previously in Figure 2.1. In these cases, misaligned expectations of value appropriation from community and enterprise members may create frictions. Avoiding those frictions demands special clarity in the rules of organisational governance and redistribution of benefits.

A final point is worth mentioning. Commons enterprises also play a political role to the extent that they may provide community members—particularly women—with opportunities for empowerment and emancipation, even if only partially so. The organisational process of setting up and developing commons enterprises, and the sense of membership derived from it, can have the same positive effects identified in the literature whereby the shared solidarity emerging from collective identifications helps create a "politics of the common good" (Singh, 2015).

Concluding remarks, principles for action, and future avenues

This chapter set about answering two questions. How can commons-based enterprises be characterised? What particular challenges do actors that engage in the development of these enterprises face? In answering the first question, the chapter has defined a commons-based enterprise as a special form of community enterprise whose primary goal is to commercialise products and services directly derived from the use of common-pool resources. The chapter analysed the interaction of two factors that affect the capacity of rural communities to set up, organise and expand commons-based enterprises: The extent of rights tenure to manage the commons and the primary driver for value generation that responds to certain characteristics of the social organisation in a community. From this— as an answer to the second question—four key challenges for the development of commons-based enterprises were identified: Expansion to wider markets, investment in organisational capacity, institutional innovation, and recombination of capital assets.

The definition of commons-based enterprises advanced in this chapter is presented as a subset of another construct—i.e., community enterprise—about which a more robust theorisation is needed. The definition is thus more of a starting point than it is a fully fledged account of what is a significantly heterogenous and locally specific phenomenon. The validity of this definition ultimately depends on the extent to which it can account for the distinctive attributes that enterprising in the context of the rural commons may comparatively exhibit. Choosing as a definitional criterion—as this chapter does—the specific type of resource from which the activities of an enterprise emanate can lead to increasing an already overcrowded universe of definitions and typologies in the specialised literature. However, the study of common-pool resources, as a sufficiently consolidated body of knowledge, provides a robust foundation and justification for advancing a resource-based definition like the one presented here.

A couple of critical considerations are needed. First, commons-based enterprises are no panacea. In the contexts analysed in this chapter, the participation of actors (other than communities, that is) who can help provide the conditions needed for developing commons-based enterprises is essential. These conditions include, inter alia, a resource base, access to markets, public goods, partnerships and networks, knowledge flows and technology. Turning the development of commons-based enterprises into a wider programmatic effort to help alleviate poverty thus demands concerted commitments from governments, NGOs, development organisations, and businesses, to name just a few. However, achieving this level of multi-sectoral collective commitment is exceptional, if possible, at all. Second, for those who see the potential advantages of entrepreneurial development as a means to lift people out of poverty, managing the expectations and aspirations of communities entails inescapable ethical considerations. Overemphasising the virtues and possibilities of entrepreneurship may lead to distorted views of what entrepreneurial development can actually achieve for communities that are often exposed to the perils of failed interventions. It can also lead to misallocation of public investment away from areas where they are most urgently needed.

Some principles for action are useful in order to take on the challenges analysed in this chapter. These principles are mostly derived from the experience shared by people who support communities in the field. The first one, informed by the reflections presented in the previous paragraph, is the necessity to *create support systems* that bring key actors from different sectors together to foster the development of commons-based enterprises. In order to make this principle workable, those support systems need not be ambitious. They may be composed of spatially localised small groups of motivated actors so that interventions can be more accurately focused. Second, *piloting interventions* is key. At the macro level, policies and programs for the promotion of entrepreneurship are needed but they often prioritise breadth over depth. In order to understand the best ways to create more impact, trying out narrowly focalised strategies before implementing wider programs is an effective way to create and share valuable knowledge and lessons. It also helps design more sensible systems of assessment and impact evaluation. Third, *promoting peer learning* offers the possibility to multiply impacts and reduce the risk of failure. Some development agencies in the region have followed a theory of change whereby commons-based enterprises that have achieved a certain level of development and sophistication are given the responsibility—as a form of reciprocal contribution for the support they received—of helping similar enterprises in earlier stages of development. This strategy has additional advantages as it can potentially increase the legitimacy of interventions.

On a theoretical level, there are three possible avenues for moving the discussion of commons-based enterprises forward. First, further elaboration on the conceptual frontiers of the construct of commons-based enterprise is necessary in order to assess its validity. Second, exploring the potential of this concept to help bridge the fields of the commons and entrepreneurship—vis à vis concepts like "institutional entrepreneurship" (Battilana et al., 2009; Garud et al., 2007) or "sustainability entrepreneurship" (Schaltegger & Wagner, 2011)—is an insufficiently explored path with potentially fruitful theoretical and practical implications. Third, advancing further in the analysis of the interplay between the organisational and political dimensions of commons-enterprise development, which entails a more thorough understanding of how issues of ownership, rights, and governance interact and the role that different political actors play in balancing this interaction, can help provide a more holistic understanding of an intrinsically diverse and complex phenomenon.

Finally, from the point of view of policy, there are also good reasons to further advance research on this topic. According to a study conducted in 13 Latin American countries, indigenous peoples and local communities own or control 23% of the total land area, compared with 18% globally (Rights and Resources Initiative, 2015). Three of these countries—Brazil, Colombia, and Mexico—account for 67% of all land recognised and owned by indigenous communities in the region. This suggests that a significant part of common-pool resources in Latin America are also owned and/or controlled by those communities. This fact alone more than justifies the importance of studying how these communities can integrate themselves into national, regional, and, eventually, global markets while helping preserve the territories and resources under their tenure. Studying the challenges of this integration is critical to understanding the development of different forms of capitals and capabilities within those communities and how those can help communities design viable livelihood strategies. This is particularly relevant in light of the well-known limitations of many Latin American countries to balance the often-contradictory demands of sustainable development and commodity-based economic growth.

Notes

1 As argued by von Benda-Beckmann, von Benda-Beckmann, and Wiber (2009), how people deal with a resource largely depends "on the other property relationships they are involved in and on the economic wealth and opportunities these embody" (p. 26). Thus, the tragedy of the commons—as conceptualised by Hardin—holds only under a specific arrangement of conditions of property, e.g., privately owned cattle that require grazing.
2 The field has not been exempt from criticism. Critics from the post-structuralist school of development point out that—in the name of resource management and conservation—commons scholars and practitioners support a programmatic agenda set out to expand and perpetuate the logics and practices of development that have long contributed to commons degradation in the first place. See, for example, the critiques of Escobar (1995) and Goldman (1997).
3 Consensus on the very definition of value creation is elusive. As argued by Lepak et al. (2007), this is particularly noticeable in the Management literature where the concept is widely used yet largely under-theorised.
4 Bridging these fields represents what some call the "next generation" questions in the commons literature, as expressed by CIFOR Senior Associate Steven Lawry (personal conversation). According to this view, promising avenues open up by shifting focus from the broad effects of collective property on conservation outcomes to the development of commons-based enterprises and their management challenges (Antinori & Bray, 2005; Baynes et al., 2015).
5 Bray et al. (2005) define these enterprises as the organisational structures that communities establish to commercialise goods and services linked to the use of community forest goods and services. Gnych et al. (2020) expand this definition to include Community Forest Institutions (CFIs) and Community User Groups (CUGs).
6 This distinction follows the conceptual difference established by Hodgson (2006) whereby an organisation is defined as a special type of institution with clear criteria to establish boundaries and distinguish membership from non-membership, principles of governance sovereignty, and chains of command delineating responsibilities. A similar distinction is followed by Friedland and Alford (1991), for whom institutions are "supraorganisational patterns" of human activity.
7 There are related concepts that explicitly incorporate conservation as a core defining characteristic. One example is Sustainability Entrepreneurship, which is defined as a specific type of entrepreneurship that significantly reduces environmental impacts. For a detailed analysis of this concept and its relationship with sustainability innovation, see Schaltegger and Wagner (2011).
8 This assumption may nevertheless be contested. Considerations other than rational choice may also be at play in the decision to preserve a common-pool resource. In fact, Ostrom's focus on rational choice theory and methodological individualism is one of the criticisms raised about her contributions to the study of cooperative behavior (see Forsyth & Johnson, 2014).

9 There are, however, significant variations. As argued by Larson and Dahal (2012), although rights may be formally sanctioned by the state, they may also be sanctioned through different institutional mechanisms such as ancestral domain or customary claims.

10 According to Besley and Ghatak (2010), there is ambiguous evidence that collective property rights achieve greater efficiency than individual property rights. Their formal analysis shows that joint ownership may be optimal in cases where the output produced with the commonly held asset is a public good as it minimises free-riding. Their results suggest that the greater the public good component in production, the more likely joint ownership will dominate individual ownership. As for the efficiency of partly private and partly public goods (as is the case with the commons), they point out that more investigation is still needed.

11 In fact, Muttenzer (2009) rightly points out that the state itself may face the same constraint in contexts where it cannot enforce hegemonic claims over certain commons while other actors can.

12 Examples of this effort include typological definitions of environmental values (Tadaki et al., 2017) and conceptualisations of social value, particularly as a defining characteristic of social enterprises (Austin et al., 2006; SEKN, 2006).

13 Some scholars argue that the analysis of the nature and particular attributes of communities that, in certain contexts, use common-pool resources demands conceptual tools that cannot be automatically transferred from mainstream fields in the study of entrepreneurship (Hindle & Lansdowne, 2005; Hindle & Moroz, 2010, cited in Hindle, 2010).

References

Agrawal, A. (2008). Sustainable Governance of Common-Pool Resources. The Contested Commons. In P. Bardhan & I. Ray (Eds.), *Conversations Between Economists and Anthropologists* (pp. 46–65). Oxford: Blackwell Publishing.

Agrawal, A., & Gibson, C. (1999). Enchantment and Disenchantment: The Role of Community in Natural Resource Conservation. *World Development*, 27(4), 629–649. https://doi.org/10.1016/S0305-750X(98)00161-2

Agrawal, A., & Ostrom, E. (2001). Collective Action, Property Rights, and Decentralization in Resource use in India and Nepal. *Politics & Society*, 29(4), 485–514. https://doi.org/10.1177%2F0032329201029004002

Ahlstrom, C. (2010). Innovation and Growth: How Business Contributes to Society. *Academy of Management Perspectives*, 24(3), 11–24. https://doi.org/10.5465/amp.24.3.11

Ambrose-Oji, B., Lawrence, A., & Stewart, A. (2015). Community Based Forest Enterprises in Britain: Two Organising Typologies. *Forest Policy and Economics*, 58, 65–74. https://doi.org/10.1016/j.forpol.2014.11.005

Anderson, A., & Jack, S. (2002). The Articulation of Social Capital in Entrepreneurial Networks: A Glue or a Lubricant? *Entrepreneurship and Regional Development*, 14, 193–210. https://doi.org/10.1080/08985620110112079

Anderson, B. (1983). *Imagined Communities: Reflections on the Origins and Spread of Nationalism*. London: Verso.

Antinori, C., & Bray, D.B. (2005). Community Forest Enterprises as Entrepreneurial Firms: Economic and Institutional Perspectives from Mexico. *World Development*, 33(9), 1529–1543. https://doi.org/10.1016/j.worlddev.2004.10.011

Arora, S., & Rommijn, H. (2012). The Empty Rhetoric of Poverty Reduction at the Base of the Pyramid. *Organization*, 19(4), 481–505. https://doi.org/10.1177%2F1350508411414294

Austin, J., Stevenson, H., & Wei-Skillern, J. (2006). Social and Commercial Entrepreneurship: Same, Different, or Both? *Entrepreneurship: Theory & Practice*, 30(1), 1–22. https://doi.org/10.1111%2Fj.1540-6520.2006.00107.x

Baker, T., & Nelson, R. (2005). Creating Something from Nothing: Resource Construction Through Entrepreneurial Bricolage. *Administrative Science Quarterly*, 50(3), 329–366. https://doi.org/10.2189%2Fasqu.2005.50.3.329

Baland, J.M., & Platteau, J.P. (1999). The Ambiguous Impact of Inequality on Local Resource Management. *World Development*, 27(5), 773–788. https://doi.org/10.1016/S0305-750X(99)00026-1

Banerjee, A.V., & Duflo, E. (2007). The Economic Lives of the Poor. *Journal of Economic Perspectives*, 21(1), 141–168. https://www.jstor.org/stable/30033705

Battilana, J., Leca, B., & Boxenbaum, E. (2009). How Actors Change Institutions: Toward a Theory of Institutional Entrepreneurship. *Academy of Management Annals*, 3(1), 65–107. https://doi.org/10.1080/19416520903053598

Baynes, J., Herbohn, J., Smith, C., Fisher, R., & Bray, D. (2015). Key Factors Which Influence the Success of Community Forestry in Developing Countries. *Global Environmental Change*, 35, 226–238. https://doi.org/10.1016/j.gloenvcha.2015.09.011

Bebbington, A. (1999). Capitals and Capabilities: A Framework for Analyzing Peasant Viability, Rural Livelihoods and Poverty. *World Development*, 27(12), 2021–2044. https://doi.org/10.1016/S0305-750X(99)00104-7

Bebbington, A. (Ed.). (2012). *Social Conflict, Economic Development and the Extractive Industry*. London: Routledge. https://doi.org/10.4324/9780203639030

Bell, C., & Newby, H. (1974). *The Sociology of Community*, London: Frank Cass and Company Limited.

Berkes, F., & Davidson-Hunt, I. (2009). Innovating Through Commons use: Community-based Enterprises. *International Journal of the Commons*, 4(1), 1–7. http://doi.org/10.18352/ijc.206

Besley, T., & Ghatak, M. (2010). Property Rights and Economic Development. In D. Rodrik & M. Rosenzweig (Eds.), *Handbook of Development Economics*, Volume 5 (pp. 4525–4595). North-Holland, The Netherlands: Elsevier.

Bonini, S., & Emerson, J. (2005). *Maximizing Blended Value—Building Beyond the Blended Value Map to Sustainable Investing, Philanthropy and Organizations*. Retrieved from http://www.blendedvalue.org/wp-content/uploads/2004/02/pdf-max-blendedvalue.pdf

Borch, O.J., Førde, A., Rønning, L., Vestrum, I.K., & Alsos, G.A. (2008). Resource Configuration and Creative Practices of Community Entrepreneurs. *Journal of Enterprising Communities: People and Places in the Global Economy*, 2(2), 100–123. https://doi.org/10.1108/17506200810879943

Boyatzis, R. (1998). *Transforming Qualitative Information: Thematic Analysis and Code Development*. Thousand Oaks, CA: SAGE.

Bray, D., Merino-Pérez, L., & Barry, D. (Eds.). (2005). *The Community Forests of Mexico. Managing for Sustainable Landscapes*. Austin, TX: University of Texas Press. https://www.jstor.org/stable/10.7560/706378

Carens, J.H. (2000). *Culture, Citizenship, and Community. Contextual Exploration of Justice as Evenhandedness.* Oxford: Oxford University Press.

Carlisle, K., & Gruby, R. (2019). Polycentric Systems of Governance: A Theoretical Model for the Commons. *Policy Studies Journal,* 47(4), 927–952. https://doi.org /10.1111/psj.12212

Casson, M., & Della Giusta, M. (2007). Entrepreneurship and Social Capital: Analyzing the Impact of Social Networks on Entrepreneurial Activity from a Rational Action Perspective. *International Small Business Journal,* 25(3), 220–244. https://doi.org/10.1177%2F0266242607076524

Cotula, L., & Mayers, J. (2009). *Tenure in REDD: Start-Point or Afterthought? Natural Resources Issues. No. 15.* London: IIED. Retrieved from https://pubs .iied.org/pdfs/13554IIED.pdf

Dacin, P., Dacin, M., & Matear, M. (2010). Social Entrepreneurship: Why we don't Need a new Theory and how we Move Forward from Here. *Academy of Management Perspectives,* 24(3), 37–57. https://www.jstor.org/stable /29764973

Dana, L.P., & Anderson, R. (2007). A Multidisciplinary Theory of Entrepreneurship as a Function of Cultural Perceptions of Opportunity. In L.P. Dana & R. Anderson (Eds.), *International Handbook of Research on Indigenous Entrepreneurship* (pp. 595–605). Cheltenham: Edward Elgar.

Elias, N. (1974). Towards a Theory of Communities. In C. Bell & H. Newby (Eds.), *The Sociology of Community.* London: Frank Cass and Company Limited.

Escobar, A. (1995). *Encountering Development: The Making and Unmaking of the Third World.* Princeton: Princeton University Press.

Fellnhofer, K. (2015). Literature Review: Investment Readiness Level of Small and Medium Sized Companies. *International Journal of Managerial and Financial Accounting,* 7(3/4), 268–284. https://doi.org/10.1504/IJMFA.2015.074904

Forsyth, T., & Johnson, C. (2014). Elinor Ostrom's Legacy: Governing the Commons and the Rational Choice Controversy. *Development and Change,* 45(5), 1093–1110. https://doi.org/10.1111/dech.12110

Frapolli, E., Ayala-Orozco, B., Oliva, M., & Smith, R. (2018). Different Approaches Towards the Understanding of Socio-Environmental Conflicts in Protected Areas. *Sustainability,* 10(7), 2240. https://doi.org/10.3390/su10072240

Fraser, N. (1995). From Redistribution to Recognition? Dilemmas of Justice in a "Post-Socialist" Age. *New Left Review,* 1(212), 68–93.

Friedland, R., & Alford, R. (1991). Bringing Society Back in: Symbols, Practices and Institutional Contradictions. In W. Powell & P. DiMaggio (Eds.), *The New Institutionalism in Organizational Analysis* (pp. 232–267). Chicago: University of Chicago Press.

Galik, C., & Jagger, P. (2015). Bundles, Duties and Rights: A Revised Framework for Analysis of Natural Resource Property Rights Regimes. *Land Economics,* 91(1), 76–90. https://doi.org/10.3368/le.91.1.76

Garud, R., Hardy, C., & Maguire, S. (2007). Institutional Entrepreneurship as Embedded Agency: An Introduction to the Special Issue. *Organization Studies,* 28(7), 957–969. https://doi.org/10.1177%2F0170840607078958

Gnych, S., Lawry, S., McLain, R., Monterroso, I., Adhikary, A. (2020). Is Community Tenure Facilitating Investment in the Commons for Inclusive and Sustainable Development? *Forest Policy and Economics,* 111, 102088. https://doi.org/10.1 016/j.forpol.2019.102088

Goldman, M. (1997). "Customs in Common": The Epistemic World of the Commons Scholars. *Theory and Society*, 26(1), 1–37. https://www.jstor.org/stable/658067

Hardin, G. (1968). The Tragedy of the Commons. *Science*, 162(3859), 1243–1248. http://doi.org/10.1126/science.162.3859.1243

Hindle, K. (2010). How Community Context Affects Entrepreneurial Process: A Diagnostic Framework. *Entrepreneurship & Regional Development*, 22(7–8), 599–647. https://doi.org/10.1080/08985626.2010.522057

Hindle, K., & Lansdowne, M. (2005). Brave Spirits on new Paths: Toward a Globally Relevant Paradigm of Indigenous Entrepreneurship Research. *Journal of Small Business and Entrepreneurship*, 18(2), 131–141. https://doi.org/10.1080/08276331.2005.10593335

Hindle, K., & Moroz, P. (2010). Indigenous Entrepreneurship as a Research Field: Developing a Definitional Framework from the Emerging Canon. *International Entrepreneurship and Management Journal*, 6, 357–385. https://doi.org/10.1007/s11365-009-0111-x

Hodgson, G. (2006). What are Institutions? *Journal of Economic Issues*, XL(1), 1–25. https://doi.org/10.1080/00213624.2006.11506879

Johannisson, B. (1988). Business Formation—a Network Approach. *Scandinavian Journal of Management*, 4(3–4), 83–99. https://doi.org/10.1016/0956-5221(88)90002-4

Johannisson, B. (1990). Community Entrepreneurship-cases and Conceptualization. *Entrepreneurship & Regional Development*, 2(1), 71–88. https://doi.org/10.1080/08985629000000006

Johannisson, B., & Monsted, M. (1997). Contextualizing Entrepreneurial Networking. *International Studies of Management & Organization*, 27(3), 109–137. https://www.jstor.org/stable/40397381

Johannisson, B., & Nilsson, A. (1989). Community Entrepreneurs: Networking for Local Development. *Entrepreneurship & Regional Development*, 1(1), 3–19. https://doi.org/10.1080/08985628900000002

Johnson, K.A., & Nelson, K.C. (2004). Common Property and Conservation: The Potential for Effective Communal Forest Management Within a National Park in Mexico. *Human Ecology*, 32(6), 703–733. https://doi.org/10.1007/s10745-004-6833-z

Julien, P. (2007). *A Theory of Local Entrepreneurship in the Knowledge Economy.* Cheltenham: Edward Elgar.

Karnani, A. (2009). Romanticising the Poor Harms the Poor. *Journal of International Development*, 21(1), 76–86. https://doi.org/10.1002/jid.1491

Kolk, A., Rivera-Santos, M., & Rufin, C. (2014). Reviewing a Decade of Research on the "Base/Bottom of the Pyramid" (BOP) Concept. *Business & Society*, 53(3), 338–377. https://doi.org/10.1177/0007650312474928

Larson, A., & Dahal, G. (2012). Forest Tenure Reform: New Resource Rights for Forest-based Communities? *Conservation and Society*, 10(2), 77–90. http://doi.org/10.4103/0972-4923.97478

Lawry, S., & McLain, R. (2012). *Devolution of Forest Rights and Sustainable Forest Management: Learning from Two Decades of Implementation.* Retrieved from: https://www.land-links.org/wp-content/uploads/2016/09/USAID_Land_Tenure_Devolution_of_Forest_Rights_and_Sustainable_Forest_Management_Volume_1.pdf

60   *Iván D. Lobo*

Lepak, D.P., Smith, K.G., & Taylor, M.S. (2007). Value Creation and Value Capture: A Multilevel Perspective. *Academy of Management Review*, 32(1), 180–194. https://doi.org/10.5465/amr.2007.23464011

Light, I. (1998). Microcredit and Informal Credit in the USA: New Strategies of Economic Development. Introduction. *Journal of Developmental Entrepreneurship*, 3(1), 1–5.

Light, I. (2005). The Ethnic Economy. In N. Smelser & R. Swedberg (Eds.), *The Handbook of Economic Sociology* (pp. 650–677). Princeton: Princeton University Press.

Light, I., & Dana, L. (2013). Boundaries of Social Capital in Entrepreneurship. *Entrepreneurship: Theory and Practice*, 37(3), 603–624. https://doi.org/10.1111%2Fetap.12016

Lin, N. (1999). Social Networks and Status Attainment. *Annual Review of Sociology*, 25, 467–487. https://www.jstor.org/stable/223513

Lipset, S.M. (2000). Values and Entrepreneurship in the Americas. In R. Swedberg (Ed.), *Entrepreneurship: The Social Science View* (pp. 110–128). Oxford: Oxford University Press.

London, T., & Hart, S. (2004). Reinventing Strategies for Emerging Markets: Beyond the Transnational Model. *Journal of International Business Studies*, 35, 350–370. https://doi.org/10.1057/palgrave.jibs.8400099

London, T., & Hart, S. (Eds.). (2011). *Next Generation Business Strategies for the Base of the Pyramid: New Approaches for Building Mutual Value*. Upper Saddle River, NJ: FT Press.

Macqueen, D. (2013). Enabling Conditions for Successful Community Forest Enterprises. *Small-scale Forestry*, 12, 145–163. https://doi.org/10.1007/s11842-011-9193-8

Macqueen, D., Andaya, E., Begaa, S., Bringa, M., Greijmans, M., Hill, T., Humphries, S., Kabore, B., Ledecq, T., Lissendja, T., Maindo, A., Maling, A., McGrath, D., Milledge, S., Pinto, F., Quang Tan, N., Tangem, E., Schons, S., & Subedi, B. (2014). *Prioritising Support for Locally Controlled Forest Enterprises*. London: IIED. Retrieved from: https://pubs.iied.org/pdfs/13572IIED.pdf

Márquez, P., Reficco, E., & Berger, G. (Eds.). (2010). *Socially Inclusive Business: Engaging the Poor Through Market Initiatives in Iberoamerica*. Cambridge, MA: Harvard University Press.

McGinnis, M.D., & Ostrom, E. (2012). Reflections on Vincent Ostrom, Public Administration, and Polycentricity. *Public Administration Review*, 72, 15–25. https://doi.org/10.1111/j.1540-6210.2011.02488.x

McMillan, D.W., & Chavis, D.M. (1986). Sense of Community: A Definition and Theory. *Journal of Community Psychology*, 14, 6–23. https://doi.org/10.1002/1520-6629(198601)14:1%3C6::AID-JCOP2290140103%3E3.0.CO;2-I

Meinzen-Dick, R.S., & Knox, A. (2001). Collective Action, Property Rights, and Devolution of Natural Resource Management: A Conceptual Framework. In R.S. Meinzen-Dick, A. Knox & M. Di Gregorio (Eds.), *Collective Action, Property Rights, and Devolution of Natural Resource Management: Exchange of Knowledge and Implications for Policy*. Feldafing: Zentralstelle für Ernährung und Landwirtschaft.

Mizik, N., & Jacobson, R. (2003). Trading off Between Value Creation and Value Appropriation: The Financial Implications of Shifts in Strategic Emphasis. *Journal of Marketing*, 67, 63–76. https://doi.org/10.1509%2Fjmkg.67.1.63.18595

Monterroso I., & Barry D. (2012). Legitimacy of Forest Rights: The Underpinnings of the Forest Tenure Reform in the Protected Areas of Petén, Guatemala. *Conservation & Society*, 10(2), 136–150. http://doi.org/10.4103/0972-4923.97486

Muttenzer, F. (2009). The Folk Conceptualisation of Property and Forest-related Going Concerns in Madagascar. In F. von Benda-Beckmann, K. von Benda-Beckmann, & M.G. Wiber (Eds.), *Changing Properties of Property* (pp. 269–292). New York: Berghahn Books. http://www.jstor.com/stable/j.ctt9qdg26.4

Ostrom, E. (1990). *Governing the Commons: The Evolution of Institutions for Collective Action*. Cambridge, UK: Cambridge University Press.

Ostrom, E. (1999). *Self-Governance and Forest Resources*. Bogor: Center for International Forestry Research. Retrieved from https://www.cifor.org/publicat ions/pdf_files/OccPapers/OP-20.pdf

Ostrom, E. (2005). *Unlocking Public Entrepreneurship and Public Economies*. WIDER Discussion Paper, No. 2005/01. Helsinki: United Nations University World Institute for Development Economics Research (UNU-WIDER). Retrieved from https://www.econstor.eu/bitstream/10419/52899/1/480453004.pdf

Ostrom, E. (2009). A General Framework for Analyzing Sustainability of Social-Ecological Systems. *Science*, 325, 419–422. http://doi.org/10.1126/science.1172133

Ostrom, E. (2010). Beyond Markets and States: Polycentric Governance of Complex Economic Systems. *American Economic Review*, 100, 641–672. https://doi.org/10.1257/aer.100.3.641

Ostrom, E., Gardner, A., & Walker, J. (1994). *Rules, Games, & Common-Pool Resources*. Ann Arbor, MI: The University of Michigan Press.

Pearce, J. (2003). *Social Enterprise in Anytown*. London: Calouste Gulbenkian Foundation.

Peredo, A.M., & Chrisman, J.J. (2006). Toward a Theory of Community-Based Enterprise. *Academy of Management Review*, 31(2), 309–328. https://www.jstor.org/stable/20159204

Peredo, A.M., & McLean, M. (2006). Social Entrepreneurship: A Critical Review of the Concept. *Journal of World Business*, 41(1), 56–65. Available at: https://ssrn.com/abstract=1197663

Peredo, A.M., Anderson, R., Galbraith, C., Honig, B., & Dana, L. (2004). Towards a Theory of Indigenous Entrepreneurship. *International Journal of Entrepreneurship and Small Business*, 1(1/2), 1–20. http://doi.org/10.1504/IJESB.2004.005374

Poteete, A., & Ostrom, E. (2004). Heterogeneity, Group Size and Collective Action: The Role of Institutions in Forest Management. *Development and Change*, 35(3), 435–462. https://doi.org/10.1111/j.1467-7660.2004.00360.x

Prahalad, C.K. (2004). *The Fortune at the Bottom of the Pyramid. Eradicating Poverty Through Profits*. Upper Saddle River, NJ: Wharton School Publishing.

Raftopoulos, M. (2017). Contemporary Debates on Social-environmental Conflicts, Extractivism and Human Rights in Latin America. *The International Journal of Human Rights*, 21(4), 387–404. http://doi.org/10.1080/13642987.2017.130 1035

Ram, M., & Jones, T. (1998). Ethnic Minorities in Business. University of Illinois at Urbana-Champaign's Academy for Entrepreneurial Leadership Historical Research Reference in Entrepreneurship. Retrieved from: https://ssrn.com/abstract=1510004

Ribot, J.C., Agrawal, A., & Larson, A.M. (2006). Recentralizing While Decentralizing: How National Governments Reappropriate Forest Resources. *World Development*, 34(11), 1864–1886. https://doi.org/10.1016/j.worlddev.2005.11.020

Rights and Resources Initiative (2015). *Who Owns the World's Land? A Global Baseline of Formally Recognized Indigenous and Community Land Rights.* Washington, DC: Rights and Resources Group. Retrieved from https://rightsandresources.org/wp-content/uploads/GlobalBaseline_complete_web.pdf

Rosa, P.J., Kodithuwakku, S., & Balunywa, W. (2006). Entrepreneurial Motivation in Developing Countries: What Does "necessity" and "opportunity" Entrepreneurship Really Mean? *Frontiers of Entrepreneurship Research*, 26(20). https://dx.doi.org/10.2139/ssrn.1310913

Salafsky, N., Cauley, H., Balachander, B., Parks, J., Margoluis, C., Bhatt, S., Encarnacion, C., Russel, D., & Margoluis, R. (2001). A Systematic Test of an Enterprise Strategy for Community-Based Biodiversity Conservation. *Conservation Biology*, 15(6), 1585–1595. https://www.jstor.org/stable/3061260

Santos, F.M. (2012). A Positive Theory of Social Entrepreneurship. *Journal of Business Ethics*, 111, 335–351. https://doi.org/10.1007/s10551-012-1413-4

Schaltegger, S., & Wagner, M. (2011). Sustainable Entrepreneurship and Sustainability Innovation: Categories and Interactions. *Business Strategy and the Environment*, 20, 222–237. https://doi.org/10.1002/bse.682

Schlager, E., & Ostrom, E. (1992). Property-Rights Regimes and Natural Resources: A Conceptual Analysis. *Land Economics*, 68(3), 249–262. http://doi.org/10.2307/3146375

Schoar, A. (2010). The Divide Between Subsistence and Transformational Entrepreneurship. *Innovation Policy and the Economy* 10: 57–81. http://doi.org/10.1086/605853

Selsky, J.W., & Smith, A. (1994). Community Entrepreneurship: A Framework for Social Change Leadership. *Leadership Quarterly*, 5(3/4): 223–226. https://doi.org/10.1016/1048-9843(94)90018-3

Shane, S. (2000). Prior Knowledge and the Discovery of Entrepreneurial Opportunities. *Organization Science*, 11(4), 448–469. https://doi.org/10.1287/orsc.11.4.448.14602

Sikor, T., He, J., & Lestrelin, G. (2017). Property Rights Regimes and Natural Resources: A Conceptual Analysis Revisited. *World Development*, 93, 337–349. https://doi.org/10.1016/j.worlddev.2016.12.032

Simão, C., & Berkes, F. (2010). Community-based Enterprises: The Significance of Partnerships and Institutional Linkages. *International Journal of the Commons*, 4(1), 183–212. http://doi.org/10.18352/ijc.133

Singh, P. (2015). *How Solidarity Works for Welfare: Subnationalism and Social Development in India*. New York: Cambridge University Press.

Social Enterprise Knowledge Network (SEKN). (2006). *Effective Management of Social Enterprises. Lessons from Businesses and Civil Society in Iberoamerica.* Cambridge, MA: Harvard University Press.

Somerville, P. (2011). *Understanding Community: Politics, Policy and Practice*, Bristol: Policy Press.

Somerville, P., & McElwee, G. (2011). Situating Community Enterprise: A Theoretical Exploration. *Entrepreneurship & Regional Development*, 23(5–6), 317–330. https://doi.org/10.1080/08985626.2011.580161

Steyaert, C. (2007). "Entrepreneuring" as a Conceptual Attractor? A Review of Process Theories in 20 Years of Entrepreneurship Studies. *Entrepreneurship & Regional Development*, 19(6), 453–477. https://doi.org/10.1080/08985620701671759

Sutter, C., Webb, J., Kistruck, G., Ketchen, D.J., & Ireland, R.D. (2017). Transitioning Entrepreneurs from Informal to Formal Markets. *Journal of Business Venturing*, 32(4), 420–442. https://doi.org/10.1016/j.jbusvent.2017.03.002

Sutter, C., Bruton, G.D., & Chen, J. (2019). Entrepreneurship as a Solution to Extreme Poverty: A Review and Future Research Directions. *Journal of Business Venturing*, 34(1), 197–214. https://doi.org/10.1016/j.jbusvent.2018.06.003

Szreter, S., & Woolcock, M. (2004). Health by Association? Social Capital, Social Theory, and the Political Economy of Public Health. *International Journal of Epidemiology*, 33(4), 650–667. https://doi.org/10.1093/ije/dyh013

Tadaki, M., Sinner, J., & Chan, K.M.A. (2017). Making Sense of Environmental Values: A Typology of Concepts. *Ecology and Society*, 22(1), 7. https://doi.org/10.5751/ES-08999-220107

Tedmanson, D., Essers, C., Dey, P., & Verduyn, K. (2015). An Uncommon Wealth. Transforming the Commons with Purpose, for People and Not for Profit! *Journal of Management Inquiry*, 24(4), 439–444. https://doi.org/10.1177%2F1056492615579791

Tracey, P., Phillips, N., & Haugh, H. (2005). Beyond Philanthropy: Community Enterprise as a Basis for Corporate Citizenship. *Journal of Business Ethics*, 58, 327–344. https://doi.org/10.1007/s10551-004-6944-x

Tripsas, M. (2009). Technology, Identity and Inertia Through the Lens of "The Digital Photography Company". *Organization Science*, 20(2), 441–460. https://doi.org/10.1287/orsc.1080.0419

UNCTAD (2014). Chapter IV: Investing in the SDGs—An Action Plan for Promoting Private Sector Contributions. In *World Investment Report 2014: Investing in the SDGs—An Action Plan*. Geneva: United Nations Conference on Trade and Development. Retrieved from http://unctad.org/en/pages/PublicationWebflyer.aspx?publicationid=937

Van Meerkerk I., Kleinhans R., & Molenveld, A. (2018). Exploring the Durability of Community Enterprises: A Qualitative Comparative Analysis. *Public Administration*, 96, 651–667. https://doi.org/10.1111/padm.12523

Viswanathan, M., Sridharan, S., & Ritchie, R. (2010). Understanding Consumption and Entrepreneurship in Subsistence Marketplaces. *Journal of Business Research*, 63(6), 570–581. https://doi.org/10.1016/j.jbusres.2009.02.023

von Benda-Beckmann, F., von Benda-Beckmann, K., & Wiber, M.G. (2009). The Properties of Property. In F. von Benda-Beckmann, K. von Benda-Beckmann, & M.G. Wiber (Eds.), *Changing Properties of Property* (pp. 1–39). New York: Berghahn Books. http://www.jstor.com/stable/j.ctt9qdg26.4

Part III

Drivers and barriers of BOP markets

3 Leadership, organisational alignment, and partnerships against economic exclusion

What do uncommon success stories have in common?

Roberto Gutiérrez

More than two decades ago, then UN Secretary General Kofi Annan invited the private sector to join in development efforts. He believed that many solutions to satisfy basic needs depended on private sector offerings. As Beinhocker and Hanauer (2014) state, prosperity is the accumulation of solutions to human problems, and companies compete to provide them. Resources flow to those who offer solutions.

Many academics have also stressed the fact that companies could address social and economic problems. Firms can step up and offer solutions. Prominent among the scholars who documented efforts for more inclusive businesses was C.K. Prahalad (2005). His image of a fortune at the bottom of the economic pyramid (BOP) captured the interest of many. However, years later many enterprises are still searching. And, as scholars we keep asking the question: Why haven't more enterprises been able to find such fortune at the BOP? In another version, Seelos and Mair ask: "If the BOP proposition is right, why then is the profit opportunity not picked up by companies on a large scale?" (2007, p. 49).

One may doubt that such fortune exists, but since some have found it in industries like microfinance, the questions have become: What have those successful firms done? And what stands in the way of others to achieve such fortune?

Rather than a mirage, as Karnani (2007) considered it, what became apparent was that the road to the economic and social benefits of including vast sectors of our societies in its economies is fraught with a myriad of barriers. Some are external (e.g., institutional voids or the very nature of BOP characteristics); others arise within the same enterprise (e.g., inadequate logistics or processes created for different conditions). Different approaches in research have sought to uncover these barriers and, thereby, find guidance to overcome them (Gutiérrez & Vernis, 2016; Reficco & Gutiérrez, 2016; Seelos & Mair, 2007).

This chapter focuses on the interventions by private firms in peripheral regions where conditions are dire compared to central locations. Operations in adverse contexts, such as urban settings of peripheral regions or the outskirts of main cities, illustrate the ways in which firms have addressed dire conditions. These are the exceptions to an otherwise weak private sector in less economically developed countries. It is enlightening to examine not only how some firms are able to circumvent difficult external conditions, but crucially, how they confront internal barriers to develop initiatives that benefit underprivileged populations.

This chapter addresses the lack of knowledge about the effects of higher-level predictors (e.g., institutional pressure) on other order outcomes (e.g., firm capabilities) and vice versa (Aguinis & Glavas, 2012). To understand how firms can overcome external and internal barriers to address economic exclusion, I chose two cases among the dozens examined by the Social Enterprise Knowledge Network (SEKN). These two multinational corporations (MNC) have a Colombian origin and work in peripheral regions. In these contexts, they have faced diverse obstacles and, to work around them, they have confronted internal challenges as well.

The following section describes the context where the field work took place. Next comes a methodology section that situates this research within the larger agenda of a hemispheric network of academics. Then, descriptive results for the two firms are presented as a preamble to three sections that detail some analytical findings. A closing section attempts to look beyond the exceptional cases.

Contexts with limited success in achieving economic inclusion

In a hemisphere where vast inequalities persist, Colombia ranks second to Haiti in economic disparities (OECD et al., 2019). Reminders of the weakness of the State are everywhere, and there has never been much faith in governments' reach in economically deprived nations. When private interests capture states or these are too weak to intervene, the fate of peripheral regions remains bleak. Some international aid, nonprofits, and a few businesses manage to step into the institutional voids.

Among many organisations, the 6,800 large firms registered in Colombia (0.4% of the total) have a considerable impact. For example, one firm, that distributes its beverages nationwide, affirms that it indirectly represents 1% of GDP. Medium-sized business amount to 6.8% of the total number of registered firms; the bulk are microenterprises. Almost 93% of Colombian organisations—1.5 out of 1.62 million—have less than ten employees (Economía Aplicada, 2019).

Social and economic conditions in Colombia reproduce the core-periphery dynamics of other capitalist societies. Colombian elites enjoy all the perks an economy can offer, and their living conditions in large cities resemble those of the privileged classes in core nations. Meanwhile, too many Colombians, especially those in peripheral regions, lack basic economic security, e.g., In the 23 largest metropolitan areas, only 54% of the economically active were formally employed (DANE, 2020). The hinterlands fare even worse, but there is no data to see the extent of their insecurities.

As long as economic exclusion prevails, basic needs such as food and shelter are erratically met. Basic utilities are a privilege in most coastal regions in Colombia.

During the COVID-19 crisis, the municipal water company in the largest coastal city boasted of connecting service to approximately 40,000 homes—15.4% were reconnected for unpaid bills—and an unknown number remain without this vital service (Acevedo, 2020). One of the better performing utilities in the entire region distributes natural gas for cooking and powering domestic appliances. There are numerous lessons to be gleaned from the experience of this corporation that has been able to overcome institutional voids and internal struggles to offer an important service.

External conditions that discourage firms from entering a new market

Certain conditions in a particular region can make operations difficult to greater or lesser degrees. For example, survival mode among potential customers, tough industry competition, or unfavorable nonmarket conditions (i.e., the space beyond economic exchanges) can inhibit companies from conducting business. It is illustrative to detail what each of these means for some of the peripheral regions in Colombia.

Underprivileged populations pose multiple challenges for firms. People at the bottom of the economic pyramid do not have the same means to buy solutions as the more privileged do, but they may eventually find ways to do so. Firms must understand what stands in the way of consumption for this population: Sometimes it is cash flow restrictions, other times, geographical barriers; it may be plain lack of awareness about a product or even an acceptance of available options.

Marketing has traditionally been a way to connect with customers. However, its instruments must be adapted to a population without the means to take advantage of an offering. For example, unawareness of a product or service results from underprivileged populations not having access to the media where ads are placed. Therefore, communication has to be specifically tailored to them. Once products or services become known, they need to be accepted by these populations. Often, they are savvy consumers, because they cannot afford to buy an underperforming product. Also, past promises can affect their willingness to consume products by certain companies.

Once its products are known and accepted, a firm has to make special efforts to make them available and affordable. Established distribution channels might be beyond the reach of the BOP. The place where these products are exhibited may be distant not only physically but also psychologically. A direct answer to the barrier of distance would be to deliver products directly to customers, but this alternative faces last-mile delivery challenges that may require the creation of new distribution channels. Last but not least, the affordability challenge brings in issues of cash flows, disposable income, informal and formal credit schemes, payment arrangements, and outstanding bills. In each dimension of the marketing mix (promotion, product, place, and price), firms need to *adapt* their approaches to a population that has very different resources and access to media and outlets.

A new marketing mix must consider awareness, acceptability, availability, and affordability (Anderson & Markides, 2007).

Industries that are embedded in weak diamonds, as Porter (1990) describes, lack economic vitality. Economic development is more akin to the frequent exchanges that happen in clusters, for example (Porter, 2000). First-mover advantages exist, indeed, but if barriers to become the first are extremely high, surmounting these might not be worth the effort. Another related deterrent for a firm is the absence of clear rules within markets (Mair & Martí, 2009).

In the *nonmarket environment,* institutional voids are among the barriers a company may encounter. These voids are defined as the absence of brokers who efficiently connect clients or consumers with providers of goods or services (Khanna & Palepu, 2010). In such situations, there is no formal or informal configuration to develop specialised brokers for four basic functions: (1) to enforce contracts; (2) to supply financial capital for business development; (3) to source human talent and partners; and (4) to provide information and public relations (Schrammel, 2014).

These voids occur when existing institutions do not provide enough guidance for the behavior of actors. Without institutional guidance, paralysis, ambiguity, or incoherent behaviors happen. When rules are disconnected from social realities, the fear of taking steps that can get you into trouble can lead to paralysis. In peripheral regions, ambiguity is the issue: Namely, there are no formal institutional agreements with enough strength to be enforced, and actors are unable to perceive any dominant institution among the several informal ones that coexist (Chaux & Haugh, 2015). Institutional voids generate reinforcing loops. For example, cities with diverse institutional arrangements accumulate inertias and important inefficiencies in the supply of certain goods such as public utilities (Antúnez & Galilea, 2003).

According to agency theory, large corporations fill in for institutions to address market failures and take advantage of the opportunities that institutional voids create (Mair et al., 2011; Webb et al., 2010). Therefore, emerging markets and their institutional voids offer considerable growth opportunities for businesses. Firms can take advantage of these opportunities if they understand how to work around institutional voids (Khanna & Palepu, 2010).

It is in these contexts that our examinations of private sector interventions took place. Dire conditions demand especial efforts, and it is enlightening to understand those few that have succeeded in offering solutions. The rest of this chapter intends to describe and analyse the solutions to economic exclusion a couple of firms have developed. But, before that, it will provide an account of the research design, sample selection, and processes followed for data collection and analyses.

Research methodology

This study is based on the case study approach. Case studies are useful for understanding the "how" and "why" of a phenomenon (Yin, 2003) and are well suited for exploring complex inter-organisational processes where comparisons are needed to explore differences or similarities within and between cases (Baxter & Jack, 2008; Eisenhardt & Graebner, 2007; Stake, 2005).

The criterion that guided this purposeful sampling (Creswell, 2013; Maxwell, 1996) was the selection of "cases from which one can learn a great deal about matters of importance and therefore worthy of in-depth study" (Patton, 2002, p. 242). These "information-rich cases" allow for valuable insights and an in-depth understanding of processes that unfold overtime.

> When the objective is to achieve the greatest possible amount of information on a given problem or phenomenon, a representative case or a random sample may not be the most appropriate strategy [...] because the typical or average case is often not the richest in information.
>
> (Flyvbjerg, 2006, p. 229)

The two cases chosen for empirical study correspond to businesses targeting low-income consumers in peripheral regions of an economically underdeveloped country. The similarities these cases share contrast with the many differences they have with ventures that have not survived. They can be considered extreme cases, the type one studies "when the purpose is to try to highlight the most unusual variation in the phenomena under investigation, rather than trying to tell something typical or average about the population in question" (Jahnukainen, 2010).

These two cases, one operating in the periphery of the country and the other one in the outskirts of its biggest cities, were chosen for three reasons: First, both companies decided to create new business models despite high market uncertainties; second, both businesses achieved a considerable scale in terms of geographical reach and numbers of customers—an uncommon attainment among BOP ventures (Bruni Celli et al.,2010); and, third, the two cases complement each other to provide maximum variation: The first one highlights how to operate in an unfavorable environment, while the second demonstrates issues related to internal challenges. It is enlightening to understand how both have been able to align profit and impact.

Both companies have been subjects of ongoing studies, in the context of a multi-year project (Márquez et al., 2010; Gutiérrez et al., 2016), thus avoiding the problems of one-off papers not embedded in ongoing research projects (Gephart 2004, p. 459). For this chapter, more qualitative and quantitative data was collected to capture the richness of the evolutionary processes within the companies and of the environments where they operate. This data included internal documents and performance indicators, as well as the perspectives of informants—both inside the companies and from key stakeholders. The semi-structured interviews, 11 in one case and 15 in the other, lasted between an hour to 90 minutes and were conducted in a span of ten years between 2007 and 2017. All were recorded and transcribed. Many questions came from a protocol elaborated collectively to study inclusive businesses (Márquez et al., 2010) and the protocol used to study their alliance portfolios (Gutiérrez et al., 2016); others were added to inquire about institutional voids and the evolution of the ventures. Transcripts were condensed into variables and constructs related to the inclusive business models created by these firms, their evolution, and the partnerships established over the years.

As for valid and reliable findings, the use of multiple sources of evidence (i.e., interviews, company documents, industry publications, archival data, and direct observation) and data triangulation reinforced construct validity. A high degree of familiarity with these cases came from using them to study other topics as part of a collective multi-year research project by the Social Enterprise Knowledge Network—SEKN (Austin et al., 2004; SEKN, 2006; Márquez et al., 2010; Reficco et al., 2018). Specifically, in relation to the two chosen cases, we have written three teaching cases (Gutiérrez et al., 2009; Trujillo & Gutiérrez, 2020; Gutiérrez, 2020), a book chapter (Schmutzler et al., 2014), and an academic article (Gutiérrez et al., 2016) and checked cited facts and interpretations with at least three executives in each company. The teaching cases themselves have been discussed in programs where company executives have participated. For reliability, we used an elaborate case study protocol and updated case study reports, which were checked by other researchers and served as documentation for our analyses.

The multiple and intertwined actions executed by two firms

If the glass looks half empty when one looks at the daunting challenges firms face in order to generate economic inclusion, it appears to be half full when examining the experiences of actual firms that have succeeded in doing so. The first part of this section describes the actions taken by a Colombian utility to face the dire conditions of one of the (economically) poorest regions in the country. The second part describes the internal changes implemented by another Colombian multinational to include a large segment of the population as customers. The descriptions help us to grasp the organisational adaptations needed to surpass external and internal barriers to economic inclusion.

A utility that defied an unfavorable external environment

In Colombia's main port on the Pacific, Buenaventura, the physical infrastructure is subpar, the State is absent in many domains, and socio-economic conditions are significantly harsher than in most cities of the country. Urban slums also exist in other large cities, but most of the population has access to basic public utilities. The conditions in Buenaventura's periphery are far worse.

Ambiguity plays an important role in the institutional voids in Buenaventura since informal groups—neighborhood associations, local gangs, and illegal actors—control parts of the city. In the absence of formal institutions, including an enduring state, convening the private sector to participate in local development is an uphill battle. Despite the existence of a variety of private, public, and community organisations, there is a dearth of specialised brokers.

The lack of *information* brokers affects the formal and informal environments in which firms operate in Buenaventura. There are few communication outlets for information to flow, which in turn is exacerbated by limited knowledge on the part of central players about local conditions. The core-periphery dynamics with all their inequities are at play in Colombia (i.e., decisions, resources, and opportunities are concentrated in the center). To make matters worse, informal information exchanges are limited by invisible barriers between neighborhoods due to violent acts carried out by illegal groups. Furthermore, the commonly held belief that the private sector only looks after its own interests impacts utilities and the development they spur.

Access to *human talent* is affected by formal and informal contexts. To begin with, formal education is subpar: Namely, few schools and scarce resources result in only 52.6% of Buenaventura's youth completing high school (López et al., 2015). Too often girls do not study because they must attend to domestic tasks. Generally, the quality of schools and informal training is poor. And, as it happens with information, invisible barriers between contending neighborhoods restrict people's mobility.

Formal demand for *financial capital* is low in Buenaventura where 35.85% of its population has unmet basic needs (López et al., 2015). High transaction costs and few brokers who lend credibility to commercial exchanges dwarf the formal supply of capital. Feedback loops inevitably emerge between scarce information, poorly qualified workers and business, and limited access to funds.

In this complex environment, relatively few private firms operate. One firm, Gases de Occidente (GdO), decided to come to the region and distribute natural gas in Buenaventura. This firm, a subsidiary of the Colombian multinational Promigas, was one of the pioneers in the natural gas sector in Latin America. Close to the region where it was incorporated in 1974, Promigas participated in a national program called Regional Gas Pipelines that was key to creating a mass market in Colombia as the century ended (Lafaurie & Mercado, 2009).

Promigas built on its experience in tough environments in the periphery to tackle the challenge of extending its service to the Pacific coast, a region that was poorer than the Caribbean coast with which they were more familiar. There was no pipeline to transport gas to Buenaventura, so GdO had to create an alternative: It used trucks to transport the gas from the last pipeline post 115 kilometers away. It took trucks more than 4 hours to cross the mountain pass in what GdO called a virtual oil pipeline. Once this option was conceived, GdO decided to adapt a program it had created to operate in a slum of Cali, the largest city in Western Colombia.

The adaptation to Buenaventura's context of "Connect with your Neighborhood" (*"Conéctate con tu barrio"*) aided the circulation of information, human talent, and financial capital. In its initial phase, GdO mapped the zones where it was going to operate, identifying actors, interactions, and invisible barriers between neighborhoods. All units of the company participated to provide an integrated depiction of the communities and territories they would service. Community leaders and government officials became brokers that helped diminish *information* voids. GdO reached out to mass media to address legitimacy concerns and prevent incoherent behaviors between formal and informal institutions. A radio broadcast was instrumental in informing communities about the public service GdO offered and in bringing the company into the communities.

GdO hired and trained *local workers* to build pipelines and other infrastructure. The corporate foundation also arrived in Buenaventura, but their work was not related to operations. The foundation partnered with other businesses and government to provide libraries and scholarships.

As for the lack of *financial capital*, GdO lobbied on behalf of consumers for government subsidies to install pipelines into their houses. Going a step further, it used its small loans platform to offer consumer credit; people bought gas appliances and paid through the billing system of GdO.

GdO adapted in other ways in Buenaventura. On the technical front, they created new connections for houses built on stilts that had to take into account ocean tides. On the social front, GdO had to complement its communication and responsible consumption campaigns with training that develop a culture of on-time payment. Finally, GdO contributed to local development by participating in collective impact initiatives coordinated by the Chamber of Commerce.

A MNC adapts to serve underprivileged populations

Working with communities and other third parties is often necessary for a firm that decides to face a complex environment. It also serves to align internal stakeholders to provide a product and create a market with a very different population. A Colombian MNC, Colcerámica (CC), that provides home improvement supplies is a clear illustration of the many adaptations that are required to reach the BOP.

CC has produced ceramic tiles since 1953. By the turn of the century, it faced stiff competition and the proposal to offer their products to low-income populations became an interesting alternative. CC had created a new line of products (with less design and cost) that appealed to these populations. The CEO of CC gave a copy of Prahalad's book, *The Fortune at the Bottom of the Pyramid: Eradicating Poverty Through Profits*, to the head of its Mass Marketing division and put him in charge of this project.

The expectation was that a new initiative, later called "Dress your House" (DYH; "*Viste tu Casa*"), could spearhead the product and market diversification processes. A new product for a different market seemed appropriate. Since nobody in CC knew about low-income consumers, the first ally invited to the project was Ashoka, a worldwide nonprofit that supported social entrepreneurs. Soon afterward, an Ashoka fellow established a network of community organisations that would convene and coordinate women willing to promote sales in one of the most peripheral areas of Bogotá. Hiring a local sales force was crucial for gaining access to households. As they went door-to-door, a mostly feminine sales force generated awareness and acceptance of CC products.

During its first half-century, CC's marketing had not reached these potential customers, and many were wary of promises from outsiders. When the firm decided to expand the reach of the local sales force, it searched for diverse allies including priests and constructors. For example, CC offered to improve the communal spaces priests used in exchange for a space on a Sunday service or program. As a company executive said, "the product is not the issue; in this market, a lot of patience and consistency is required to create trust and legitimacy among community members."

A few months into operation, CC opened a Service Center in the neighborhood. It was important for families to see the product and for CC to have a training space to sell and install it. Local women continued to sell and customers picked up the product at the nearest hardware stores. This first distribution arrangement did not work well because customers had no vehicle to carry boxes of heavy tiles. After many cost calculations and discussions about the feasibility of using small trucks on unpaved and steep streets, CC decided to deliver its product at the door of its customers. After rounds of trial and error, this last distribution scheme solved the availability issue.

Addressing the affordability issue was another challenge. At first, sales were minimal even though the product was much cheaper. Sales only picked up when CC started to offer credit to its customers. The company created its own credit score and managed a financing scheme. But, as sales grew along with accounts payable, CC realised it had to find an ally that knew about consumer credit. So, they turned to utilities that had been using their billing platforms to offer credit to their clients, initially for appliances but later for many other products and services. Eventually one of these utilities, Natural Gas, worked out an agreement in which its customers could buy CC's products through monthly installments.

To fulfill orders, CC had to change the handling of products: Picking them up from warehouse stacks became extremely laborious because quantities were much smaller than those managed for other types of customers. The time that products were kept in the catalog was extended from two to three years, so that low-income families could take their time to remodel their whole house. This decision affected inventory levels. Distribution was also upended. Distribution channels to low-income populations are labor intensive. For CC, scaling operations meant an increase in labor requirements and costs. The cost of goods sold (COGS) increased in tandem with sales, so productivity was sought through the adoption of new information systems and the training and empowerment of the sales force.

All of these activities required some in CC to do things differently. Managing sales personnel in this initiative had its own processes; customer financing became an issue; new handling and several distribution channels were attempted, and other marketing techniques came in handy. Each link in the value chain had effects on others, and delays or problems easily escalated. According to its director, DYH was "a small company within a large firm." The coexistence of two systems was not easy, and adjustments were made in many units.

Within the firm, those who were not in contact with DYH were unaware of it. Therefore, after several years of operation, DYH made a video filmed in three large cities (Bogotá, Cartagena, and Cali), which showed its scope and accomplishments. CC's employees became aware of the differences between DYH and their units and were more motivated to work with it. Some even declared they were in love with the program, due to its impact.

Interestingly, CC's executives believed that the largest impact of this initiative was the effect of hiring local sales promoters. It was only some years into the initiative that it became clear to them that the largest impact was achieved through product sales. Furthermore, low-income customers had improved their homes accruing three clear benefits: Better health, higher self-esteem, and an increase in property value.

Overcoming external and internal obstacles

Although change requires more than understanding someone else's experience, it can start there. Organisational learning and change do include examining cases like the ones described above, but they also require adapting and testing those lessons in a new environment. It is useful, then, to highlight the mechanisms GdO and CC used to overcome the obstacles posed by an unsupportive environment and the changes in conventional ways made within the firm to create a new market for some of its products.

An initial consideration is the interconnectedness between what happens beyond organisational borders and what happens inside the firm. The outside world recognises a firm as one entity; it considers it as a single organisation, even though it can be internally split about a particular issue or it can have multiple faces—the one belonging to its employees and those belonging to its founders or subcontractors. For better and for worse, a firm's legitimacy is tied to the reputation of those who are associated with it. The strength of a firm's response to certain institutional voids depends not only on its degree of internal agreement but also on the cohesiveness of its value network (i.e., its partners in producing value) and its other alliances. Without alliances, GdO and CC would not have thrived in the nonmarket space, nor would they have been able to create a market or develop their initiatives.

Alliances have a special role in developing new markets. Firms use partnership strategies to access resources outside their boundaries (Dyer & Singh, 1998; Gulati et al., 2000). A specific analysis of the alliances used by CC and Promigas reveal that "in both cases, resource commitments for partnerships increase as part of a focused exploration, and then as the exploration phase gives way to exploitation. In the process, cross-sector partnerships (prevalent in the probing phase) are replaced by same-sector ones" (Gutiérrez et al., 2016).

Both firms reached out to cross-sector partners to develop native capability and gather market intelligence. In particular, partnerships with civil society organisations promoted and gained acceptance for their products; alliances with private firms provided access and affordability. One community leader recognised the company's efforts: "CC would not have gotten to where it is if it had relied on Marketing and Salespeople alone; bringing in social and community experts allowed them to reach out and show people that all these efforts were worthwhile."

After the exploration stages, both firms developed *ad hoc* business models to serve low-income populations through heterogeneous alliance portfolios. Once they decided to scale up, efficiency and control requirements increased, and they trimmed these portfolios. CC replaced some cross-sector with same-sector partnerships and internalised some of the functions performed by civil society organisations. Arms-length relations with commercial operators replaced the rich two-way information exchanges of initial cross-sector partnerships. Contrary to the need for horizontal partnerships between companies and nonprofit/grass roots organisations in all stages of the venture (London et al., 2010; London & Hart, 2010; London, 2007), the two cases place this need at the initial stages of a venture.

For any company to operate in a peripheral setting, the external challenges of coordinating with allies to face institutional voids are matched by the internal tensions of facing contrasting logics, pursuing social and economic goals, and attempting exploitation after an exploration phase. All these require, as Simsek and colleagues put it, an "organisation's ability to perform differing and often competing strategic acts at the same time" (2009, p. 865).

The coexistence of a mainstream business (targeted to mass markets) and a venture targeted to the BOP is difficult. As the CC case attests, the organisational culture, incentives, and processes tailored to one segment do not suit the other. Straddling between two business models is costly (Porter, 1980), and large firms with BOP ventures face challenges of coordination and centralisation (Alonso et al., 2008). An ambidextrous ability to simultaneously pursue competing goals helped those organisations to minimise straddling costs.

From the three ways in which firms develop organisational ambidexterity, CC and GdO chose a structural mechanism to cope with competing demands (Adler et al., 1999; Tushman & O'Reilly, 1996). They structurally separated BOP operations (i.e., created physically and culturally separate units with different incentive systems and managerial teams) from those of mainstream markets. Initially, BOP ventures explored new asset configurations. As they developed resources and competencies, they kept the BOP unit independent and moved it to an exploitation phase.

The protective role of structural separation has been recognised in the literature (Raisch & Birkinshaw, 2008, Hahn et al., 2016). The role of an independent unit transforming the main business is less documented. The DYH program allowed CC to understand different value propositions for groups that they did not have on their radar. Its distribution channels have become more sophisticated, and today, they are able to satisfy other customers.

Conflicts along the way

Doing good does not keep a company immune from conflicts. Unwarranted attacks can come from government agencies or civil society. As the cases of GdO and CC show, these threats can materialise at any time.

Lawrence (2010) has studied conflicts that arise in nonmarket environments. She devised four alternatives that emerged from the intersection between the power of a firm, its resource dependency, and the urgency to find solutions: Namely, wage a fight, wait, withdraw, and work it out. GdO engaged in the latter when Council members in Buenaventura accused it of not having the appropriate operating licenses. The firm's operations had disrupted some clientele relationships, and the accusations were an attempt to reinstate those relationships.

Party politics, ideological debates about private gains and public service, and petty political interests can pose significant risks for public utilities. GdO avoided any political affiliation to protect its investments and gain wide community acceptance for its service (something none of the other public utilities had managed to do). In order to further shield their operations from political attacks, GdO improved its systems to avoid billing errors, upheld its commitment to hire locally, promoted local economic development, and highlighted success stories of improved quality of life in different social media.

Another type of conflict brewed as CC moved to an exploitation phase with its DYH venture. This conflict was rooted in institutional change: Namely, nonprofit organisations in charge of creating social value fear the encroachment of private firms in that space. Civil society organisations, especially previous partners, criticised CC for pursuing economic gains with DYH. CC dropped some cross-sector partnerships and gave prominence to same-sector ones as it sought efficiency and control in its operations. Those left behind argued moral imperatives, but CC signaled that without the creation of economic value, DYH would remain a small program in a philanthropic corner. Once CC gathered enough experience and market intelligence, it standardised processes and sought control to exploit its standing in a market, either by internalising portions of the value system or keeping their portfolios as homogeneous as possible. Acting as a social enterprise that pursues economic and social goals, CC faced external conflicts—"Social enterprises can be seen as threatening to the dominance of incumbent organisations that enact institutionalised forms" (Battilana & Lee, 2014, p. 411)—and internal disagreements. The latter is discussed in the following section.

Persistence and support

Motivation and support are key to facing complex challenges and prevailing. Does it make a difference that the first impulse is altruistic or utilitarian? There is a saying: "It doesn't matter if a cat is black or white so long as it catches mice."

Both GdO and CC fulfill their mission and simultaneously create social and economic value. Both also discovered that it was not an easy feat. Other firms with similar scaling challenges decide to keep their BOP ventures small (Gutiérrez & Vernis, 2016).

Support was crucial, from the C-suite in the case of GdO and from a member of the founding family in the case of CC. According to its CEO, despite internal disagreements it would have been quite unpopular to terminate DYH. Initially, it had backing from the Board of Directors; in time, DYH became well-known and highly regarded at different levels of the firm. According to one CC executive, "if we had calculated profits and losses from day one, we would still be discussing whether or not to start this venture."

Jaen and colleagues have highlighted the importance of

> leaders who succeeded in building inclusive ventures at the BOP, in contexts marked by institutional voids, with formal markets weakly structured or nonexistent. Building a viable business, under those circumstances, entailed two tasks: first, imagining what is possible, and second, turning that vision into a reality.
>
> (2020)

Leaders acting as catalyzers and innovators ensure buy-in and commitment from all kinds of stakeholders. Among them, investors' participation has been characterised as patient capital (Reficco & Márquez, 2012). In the case of CC, for example, only in its seventh year of operation did DYH become profitable.

It is telling that support from the corporate foundation did not exist. Colombian society, as throughout Latin America, still regards social and economic issues as removed from one another; corporate foundations rarely participate in business operations. Both Promigas and CC have corporate foundations that were typical in this sense as they observed from a distance. One director of the Corona Foundation admitted she did not understand what CC was up to. Both companies were a *rara avis*, treading in a territory where few others had dared: Firms were expected to focus on business, and social issues were to be addressed by foundations and other civil society organisations.

Multilateral agencies have played a unique role in Latin American societies where social and economic issues continue to be divorced. On occasion, financial partners and multilateral agencies have been the ones to show governments the type of support needed. The World Bank and the Inter-American Development Bank, for example, designed programs to support the private sector as it ventured into specific social ventures. During Promigas' first wave of expansion into peripheral areas, the World Bank and the Dutch Embassy became financial partners to ease households' payment of the connection fee (approximately 650 USD) to the gas network for millions of low-income consumers (Gutiérrez et al., 2016). When GdO decided to provide service in Buenaventura, it had to find government subsidies to lower this entrance barrier for low-income households.

Lessons to build hope: Looking beyond unique cases

The 2020 pandemic has shown us the interconnectedness of our endeavors. Although the social underpinnings of private enterprises have become extremely visible, it remains to be seen if companies will expand their operations to address the needs of the economically excluded. Examples like the ones presented in this chapter help to expand awareness and take into account the many roadblocks along the way. In particular, Latin America needs institutional changes that privilege sustainability.

This study examines the interventions by firms that have successfully aligned profit and impact. It presents the findings of two cases from a larger set of case studies. As Santos and his colleagues (2015) anticipated, this alignment has strengthened their sustainability and contributed to Colombian development. Unfortunately, it is not an easy endeavor because inclusive businesses are not simply more of the same recipe. New business models must respond to the specific characteristics and needs of low-income populations, and they will inevitably collide with established ones.

This was more acute in CC, where the conventional model was separate from the one that incorporated distinct products, inventory, credit, and distribution channels. However, the firm was able to develop the capacity for organisational ambidexterity that allowed it the exploration and exploitation that economic inclusion entails. "If an organisation neglects exploration, it is giving up the future; if it focuses entirely on exploration, it risks short-term survival" (Reficco & Gutiérrez, 2016, p. 4). Structural separation, as a mechanism to become ambidextrous, did well to allow the coexistence of very different business models in CC.

Most attention has gone to finding a business model because the model that works for privileged populations does not translate to low-income segments. Attempting to do business with the latter has been a challenge that most companies have foregone. However, if capitalism is to survive as a system, it must go beyond the 15% of the population that has appropriated most of its benefits (Wallerstein, 1995). As is the case with democracy, capitalism might not be the ideal system, but it is what we have. Rather than destroying the system, we must rectify the conditions that hinder the quality of life for most people in our societies.

The search for profitable, replicable, and scalable business models for BOP ventures is now easier since others have shown that it is possible. This organisational mimicry is one way that GdO and CC have had an impact. Other utilities and home improvement suppliers have started to consider serving economically excluded populations. However, it will not be easy for them to catch up. According to CC executives, in 2020 they were so far ahead that they did not mind allowing their name to appear on the second teaching case written about their experience (Trujillo & Gutiérrez, 2020), something they did not want when the first teaching case was published (Gutiérrez et al., 2009).

Some years ago, social value creation might not have been in sight, at least not at the levels that have been attained lately. In the beginning, CC aimed to have an inclusive distribution network. In time, it discovered it could create much more social value through its product than simply by hiring underprivileged saleswomen. The health, self-esteem, and economic benefits from the sale of its products have now reached more than a million Colombians. The venture only became profitable after six years of trials and struggles. Scale was finally achieved after learning from mistakes and in spite of criticisms, the result of balancing acts and tradeoffs between social and economic dimensions.

This chapter asked about the different efforts that these exceptional cases made to fulfill the BOP promise. In sum, they combined systemic, organisational, and individual responses. Support from these different levels makes BOP ventures possible. Leaders need to persist with a vision and support, inching towards inclusive business models. At the system level, where institutional voids prevail, a company must work with others to create a market. Early adopters will find it difficult to gain that first-mover advantage; those that come later benefit from the transition to formality in labor and commercial agreements.

The main contribution of this chapter is to address this combined imperative: Opportunities emerge as firms combine individual leadership, organisational alignment (allowing for loosely coupled business models), and collective pursuits. Leading, aligning, and partnering are required for BOP challenges. One without the other two cannot overcome the difficulties of economic exclusion.

Each one of these requirements for economic inclusion by a firm has been addressed by separate literatures. The tendency for responsible leadership, organisational alignment/strategy, and institutional literatures to gain knowledge from in-depth studies runs counter to the need to branch out and combine insights.

Two cases are, indeed, a limited sample. An in-depth analysis is possible with such a limited number of cases, but an exploration into the efforts of more organisations is required. As the number of organisations with BOP ventures increases, it is worth tracing the characteristics of institutional change. Since organisations can also be nonprofits that create income-earning ventures, comparative analyses with for-profits can offer a glimpse into the nature of the obstacles they confront. They are bound to face most of the barriers described in this chapter, but are there others distinctly related to their nonprofit nature?

Another limitation of the empirical study reported in this chapter is its focus on large companies. Start-ups have fewer resources and capabilities to find a replicable, profitable, and scalable business model. However, start-up models do not have to coexist with an established one. At the system level, start-ups rely more on partnerships for their operations than do larger firms (Rothaermel & Deeds, 2004). Thus, there is another research opportunity to compare ventures between companies of different sizes. Can the dynamism of social entrepreneurship provide significantly more impact than the isolated cases large companies have offered until now? Are the inertia of large firms and their ingrained interests more onerous than start-ups' lack of resources?

These two sets of inquiries are related to the nature and size of the organisations involved in BOP ventures, and they can provide insights into the institutional changes we are undergoing. The sooner we recognise and engage in combining social and economic dimensions, and exploring and exploiting the opportunities that emerge, the better and more robust our organisational attempts at sustainability will be. But, beyond the content of this research, we need an approach that combines leadership, organisational, and systemic considerations. To make a dent in escalating economic inclusion requires all these combinations.

References

Acevedo, T. (2020). Ejemplo para el mundo. *El Espectador*, 3 de mayo [access on May 21, 2020, to https://www.elespectador.com/opinion/ejemplo-para-el-mundo-columna-917501].

Adler, P.S., Goldoftas, B., & Levine, D.I. (1999). Flexibility versus efficiency? A case study of model changeovers in the Toyota production system. *Organization Science*, *10*, 43–68.

Aguinis, H., & Glavas, A., 2012. What we know and don't know about corporate social responsibility: A review and research agenda. *Journal of Management* 38(4), 932–968.

Alonso, R., Dessein, W., & Matouschek, N. (2008). When does coordination require centralization? *American Economic Review*, 98(1), 145–179.

Anderson, J., & Markides, C. (2007). Strategic innovation at the base of the economic pyramid. *MIT Sloan Management Review*, 49(1), 83–88.

Antúnez, I., & Galilea, S. (2003). Servicios públicos urbanos y gestión local en América Latina y el Caribe: Problemas, metodologías y políticas. *CEPAL, Serie Medio Ambiente y Desarrollo*, N°69, septiembre.

Austin, J.E., & SEKN Research Team. (2004). *Social Partnering in Latin America: Lessons Drawn from Collaborations of Businesses and Civil Society Organizations.* Boston: David Rockefeller Center for Latin American Studies, Harvard University, and Inter-American Development Bank.

Battilana, J., & Lee, M. (2014). Advancing research on hybrid organizing—insights from the study of social enterprises. *Academy of Management Annals*, 8(1), 397–441.

Baxter, P., & Jack, S. (2008). Qualitative case study methodology: Study design and implementation for novice researchers. *Qualitative Reports*, 13, 544–559.

Beinhocker, E., & Hanauer, N. (2014). Redefining capitalism. *McKinsey Quarterly*, September.

Bruni Celli, J., & González, R. (2010). Negocios rentables con impacto social. *Debates IESA*, *15*(3).

Chaux, M.D., & Haugh, H. (2015). How institutional voids shape economic opportunities in refugee camps. *Academy of Management Proceedings*, *2015*(1), 17965.

Creswell, J.W. (2013). *Research Design: Qualitative, Quantitative and Mixed Methods Approaches*, Sage.

DANE-Departamento Administrativo Nacional de Estadística. (2020). "Empleo informal y seguridad social". https://www.dane.gov.co/index.php/estadisticas-por-tema/mercado-laboral/empleo-informal-y-seguridad-social (access on August 10, 2020).

Dyer, H.D., & Singh, H. (1998). The relational view: Cooperative strategy and sources of inter-organizational competitive advantage. *Academy of Management Review*, 23(4), 660–679.

Economía Aplicada. (2019). "2019: ¿Cuántas empresas hay en Colombia?" http://economiaaplicada.co/index.php/10-noticias/1493-2019-cuantas-empresas-hay-en-colombia (access on August 10, 2020).

Eisenhardt, K.M., & Graebner, M.E. (2007). Theory building from cases: Opportunitiesand challenges. *Academy of Management Journal*, 50, 25–32.

Flyvbjerg, B. (2006). Five misunderstandings about case-study research. *Qualitative Inquiry*, 12,219–245.

Gephart, R. P., Jr. (2004). Qualitative Research and the Academy of Management Journal [Editorial]. *Academy of Management Journal*, 47(4), 454–462. https://doi.org/10.5465/AMJ.2004.14438580.

Gulati, R., Nohria, N., & Zaheer, A. (2000). Strategic networks. *Strategic Management Journal*, 21(5), 203–215.

Gutiérrez, R. (2020). *Promigas y Gases de Occidente.* Boston: Harvard Business School Cases.

Gutiérrez, R., Márquez, P., & Reficco, E. (2016). Configuration and development of alliance portfolios: A comparison of same-sector and cross-sector partnerships. *Journal of Business Ethics*, 135, 55–69.

Gutiérrez, R., Trujillo, D.M., Orozco, L.E., & Thiell, M. (2009). *Ceramics of Costaragua: The Challenges of Selling to Low- Income Citizens.* Boston: Harvard Business School Cases.

Gutiérrez, R., & Vernis, A. (2016). Innovations to serve low-income citizens: When corporations leave their comfort zones. *Long Range Planning*, 49, 283–297.

Hahn, T., Pinkse, J., Preuss, L., & Figge, F. (2016). Ambidexterity for corporate social performance. *Organization Studies*, 37(2), 213–235.

Jaen, M.H., Reficco, E., & Berger, G. (2020). Does integrity matter in BOP ventures? The role of responsible leadership in inclusive supply chains. *Journal of Business Ethics*, https://doi.org/10.1007/s10551-020-04518-0.

Jahnukainen, M. (2010). Extreme cases. In Wiebe, E., Durepos, G., & Mills, A.J. (Eds.), *Encyclopedia of Case Study Research* (pp. 378–379). Thousand Oaks, CA: SAGE.

Karnani, A. (2007). The mirage of marketing to the bottom of the pyramid. *California Management Review*, 49(4), 90–111.

Khanna, T., & Palepu, K. (2010). *Winning in Emerging Markets: A Roadmap for Strategy and Execution.* Boston: Harvard Business Press.

Lafaurie, L.F., & Mercado, A.I. (2009). *Promigas S.A.: 30 años de historia.* Bogotá: Facultad de Administración.

Lawrence, A.T. (2010). Managing disputes with nonmarket stakeholders: Wage a fight, withdraw, wait, or work it out. *California Management Review*, 53(1), 90–113.

London, T. (2007). *Improving the Lives of the Poor? Assessing the Impacts of Base-of-the-Pyramid Ventures.* Michigan: William Davidson Institute/Stephen M. Ross School of Business, University of Michigan.

London, T., Anupindi, R., & Sheth, S. (2010). Creating mutual value: Lessons learned from ventures serving base of the pyramid producers. *Journal of Business Research*, 63, 582–594.

London, T., & Hart, S.L. (2010). *Next Generation Business Strategies for the Base of the Pyramid: New Approaches for Building Mutual Value.* Upper Saddle River, NJ: FT Press.

López Peña, N., Rojas Andrade, G.A., & Iturralde Sánchez, M.A. (2015). *Buenaventura: Entre el desarrollo portuario y la crisis humanitaria.* Bogotá: Uniandes.

Mair, J., & Martí, I. (2009). Entrepreneurship in and around institutional voids: A case study from Bangladesh. *Journal of Business Venturing*, 24(5), 419–435.

Mair, J., Martí, I., & Ventresca, M.J. (2011). Building inclusive markets in Rural Bangladesh: How intermediaries work institutional voids. *Academy of Management Journal*, 55(4), 819–850.

Márquez, P., Reficco, E., & Berger, G. (2010). *Socially Inclusive Business: Engaging the Poor Through Market Initiatives in Iberoamerica.* Cambridge, MA: Harvard University David Rockefeller Center for Latin American Studies and Inter-American Development Bank.

Maxwell, J.A. (1996). *Qualitative Research Design: An Interactive Approach, AppliedSocial Research Methods Series,* vol. 41, Thousand Oaks, CA: SAGE.

OECD et al. (2019). *Latin American Economic Outlook 2019: Development in Transition.* Paris: OECD Publishing.

Patton, M.Q. (2002). *Qualitative Research & Evaluation Methods.* Thousand Oaks, CA: SAGE.

Porter, M. (1980). *Competitive Strategy: Techniques for Analyzing Industries and Competitors.* New York: Free Press.

Porter, M. (1990). The competitive advantage of nations. *Harvard Business Review,* March-April.

Porter, M. (2000). Location, competition, and economic development: Local clusters in a global economy. *Economic Development Quarterly,* 14(1), 15–34.

Prahalad, C.K. (2005). *The Fortune at the Bottom of the Pyramid: Eradicating Poverty Through Profits.* Upper Saddle River, NJ: Wharton School Publishing.

Raisch, S., & Birkinshaw, J. (2008). Organizational ambidexterity: Antecedents, outcomes, and moderators. *Journal of Management, 34,* 375–409.

Reficco, E., & Gutiérrez, R. (2016). Organizational ambidexterity and the elusive quest for successful implementation of BOP ventures. *Organization & Environment,* 29(4), 461–485.

Reficco, E., Gutiérrez, R., Jaén, M.H., & Auletta, N. (2018). Collaboration mechanisms for sustainable innovation. *Journal of Cleaner Production,* 203, 1170–1186.

Reficco, E., & Márquez, P. (2012). Inclusive networks for building BOP markets. *Business and Society,* 51(3), 512–554.

Rothaermel, F.T., & Deeds, D.L. (2004). Exploration and exploitation alliances in biotechnology: A system of new product development. *Strategic Management Journal,* 25(3), 201–221.

Santos, F., Pache, A.C., & Birkholz, C. (2015). Making hybrids work: Aligning business models and organizational design for social enterprises. *California Management Review,* 57(3), 36–58.

Schmutzler, J., Gutiérrez, R., Reficco, E., & Márquez. (2014). Evolution of an alliance portfolio to develop an inclusive business. In Seitanidi, M. & A. Crane (Eds.), *Social Partnerships and Responsible Business: A Research Handbook* (pp. 172–188). London: Routledge.

Schrammel, T. (2014). *Clusters As an Instrument to Bridge Institutional Voids in Transition Economies Lessons Learned from Southeast Europe.* New York: Gabler.

Seelos, C., & Mair, J. (2007). Profitable business models and market creation in the context of deep poverty: A strategic view. *Academy of Management Perspectives,* 21(4), 49–63.

SEKN. (2006). *Effective Management in Social Enterprise: Lessons from Business and Civil Society Organizations in Iberoamerica.* Boston, USA: David Rockefeller Center for Latin American Studies, Harvard University, and Inter-American Development Bank.

Simsek, Z. (2009). Organizational ambidexterity: Towards a multilevel understanding. *Journal of Management Studies, 46,* 597–624.

Stake, R.E., (2005). Qualitative case studies. In Denzin, N.K., & Lincoln, Y.S. (Eds.), *The SAGE Handbook of Qualitative Research*. Thousand Oaks: SAGE.

Trujillo, D.M., & Gutiérrez, R. (2020). *Dress Your Home*. Boston: Harvard Business School Cases.

Tushman, M.L., & O'Reilly, C.A. (1996). Ambidextrous organizations: Managing evolutionary and revolutionary change. *California Management Review*, 38(4), 8–29.

Wallerstein, I. (1995). *Historical Capitalism with Capitalist Civilization*. London: Verso.

Webb, J.W., Kicstruck, G.M., Ireland, R.D., & Ketchen, D.J. (2010). The entrepreneurship process in base of the pyramid markets: The case of multinational enterprise/nongovernment organization alliances. *Entrepreneurship: Theory & Practice*, May, 555–581.

Yin, R.K. (2003). *Case Study Research: Design and Methods*. Beverly Hills, CA: SAGE.

Part IV

Design, integration, innovation, and change of BOP markets

4 Scaling up Inclusive Distribution Networks (IDNs)

Inertias against sustainability

Diana Trujillo and Adriana Puerto

Sustainable Business Models (SBMs) take into account the needs of all stakeholders and the natural environment (Abdelkafi and Tauscher, 2016; Bocken et al., 2014; Stubbs and Cocklin, 2008). These business models (BMs) consider not only the value created but also the value destroyed and uncaptured (Bocken et al., 2014; Yang et al., 2017). In this chapter, we analyse the business models of five Inclusive Distribution Networks (IDNs) created by large multinational corporations operating in five Latin American countries. IDNs are distribution channels that incorporate cross-sector partnerships and strategic individual partners from the BOP who form part of a product and service sales network within their communities (Camenzuli and McKague, 2015; Dolan, 2012; Viswanathan and Sridharan, 2009). We use this framework to analyse changes in these IDN business models by comparing their components at the start-up phase to those resulting from adaptations made for successful scale-up. We consider a scale-up to be successful when the initiative reaches massive numbers of consumers. We then identify the effects of the adjusted business models on all value creation dimensions of sustainability: Economic, social, interaction, and environmental.

Our findings contradict the positive bias of research on IDNs that considers these business models as very successful. In scaling up BOP solutions, those BMs that began as inclusive, open, and cross-sectoral changed to operating under a pure market logic to achieve economic success. We show how IDNs, as they evolve toward achieving financial sustainability, strengthen the economic aspects of the value proposition, creating greater benefits for Multinational Corporations (MNCs), while the adjusted business models weaken the social components of the value proposition for female beneficiaries, BOP consumers, and the organisational ecosystem and decidedly ignore the model's negative environmental effects. In the sample, cross-sector ecosystems that did not make these adjustments went bankrupt. A particularly interesting aspect of the evolution of these BMs is that, despite the changes in the BM after scale-up, anchor organisations used decoupling mechanisms (Meyer and Rowan, 1977; Whiteman and Cooper, 2016) to continue legitimising the IDN as a sustainable business model, shared value model, or Corporate Social Responsibility (CSR) initiative.

Our contributions deepen the understanding of the mechanisms whereby BOP solutions gain efficiencies that lead to increased economic value creation for

MNCs. We also contribute by identifying the inertias in the distribution field that affect sustainability. Finally, we expand the research on IDNs and Cross-Sector Business Models for Sustainability by describing the difficulties that arise when ecological concerns are incorporated into BOP solutions.

Inclusive distribution networks as Cross-Sector Business Models for Sustainability

Since the literature does not explicitly provide a descriptive approach to Cross Sector Business Models for Sustainability, we follow Bocken et al. (2014), Bocken et al. (2015), and Dembek et al. (2018), who describe nine archetypes that categorise and explain Sustainable Business Models. These archetypes include, among others: Developing scale-up solutions; repurposing the business for society/the environment (Bocken et al., 2014, 2015); and BOP solutions or inclusive businesses for BOP populations (Dembek et al., 2018). In this chapter, we focus on one of said BOP business models: IDNs that have been used to reach vulnerable populations—entrepreneurs and final consumers (Camenzuli and McKague, 2015, p. 71)—and that recognise poor people as "creative entrepreneurs and value-conscious consumers" (Prahalad, 2005).

Scholars have reached agreements about the emergence of IDNs (Chikweche and Fletcher, 2011; Christensen et al., 2010a); sustainability (Camenzuli and McKague, 2015; Christensen et al., 2010b); beneficiaries' profiles (Bosma et al., 2009; Dolan, 2012; Norton, 1988); financing and working capital (Esko et al., 2013; Gold et al., 2013; Jones, 2008; Vachani and Smith, 2008; Van Kirk, 2010); the model's logistics and strategies (Chatnani, 2010; Daley, 2014; Gold et al., 2013; Sodhi and Tang, 2013); and motivational strategies for beneficiaries (Dolan et al., 2012; Gimenez et al., 2012; Hahn and Gold, 2014; Pullman et al., 2009; Rivera-Santos and Rufin, 2010; Webb et al., 2010).

However, literature on IDN outcomes and results shows two different views. On the one hand, there are authors who focus on the positive effects of IDNs. They see IDNs as market-based, scalable solutions aimed at alleviating poverty and bringing economic empowerment to their beneficiaries (Dolan, 2012; Dolan et al., 2012; Kistruck et al., 2011; Smith, 2008; Wankel, 2008). Identified benefits for companies include: Accessing knowledge regarding BOP markets (Chikweche and Fletcher, 2011; Hahn and Gold, 2014); increasing the share of BOP markets (Chikweche and Fletcher, 2011); increasing bargaining power with retailers (Chikweche and Fletcher, 2011); creating a source for firms' competitive advantage and reputation (Vachani and Smith, 2008); and leveraging social capital in communities, such as relationships, traditions, and leadership. Civil Society Organisations (CSOs) who participate in these networks can enhance their impact on BOP segments by lowering delivery costs and scalability (Smith, 2008). Governmental agencies improve the use of resources, increase their network coverage (Vachani and Smith, 2008), and improve clients/citizens' quality of life (Smith, 2008). Consumers increase their access to products in convenient ways (Chikweche and Fletcher, 2011). Micro-sellers reduce start-up costs with less risk than through traditional entrepreneurship (Christensen et al., 2010a). They also gain access to convenient and flexible working capital (Mair and Marti, 2012) and to the firm's marketing and sales resources, such as ads, catalogs, and advertising material (Chelekis and Mudambi, 2010). Micro-sellers develop business abilities, self-esteem, and motivation (Chatnani, 2010; Chelekis and Mudambi, 2010; Christensen et al., 2010a; Dolan, 2012), as well as empowerment and independence (Chelekis and Mudambi, 2010; Chikweche and Fletcher, 2011). These sellers can also rely on the legitimacy and social capital of non-governmental organizations (NGOs) and companies to safely distribute their products and increase their communities' trust in them (Tsai and Ghoshal, 1998, in Hahn and Gold, 2014, p. 1329).

On the other hand, various studies take a more critical approach by considering the challenges and difficulties of implementing IDNs. Some studies focus on changes in the cross-sector alliances portfolio as IDNs evolve (Gutiérrez et al., 2016) and on the difficulties of maintaining both a traditional business model and an IDN model within the same organisation, which requires organisational ambidexterity (Reficco and Gutiérrez, 2016). Others have addressed the deficiencies of shared value models (Crane et al., 2014) and the inequalities promoted by firms in the creation, appropriation, and distribution of value (Bapuji et al., 2018). Other works highlight the incompatibility between the IDNs' actual outcomes and the intended norms that result in decoupling (Crane et al., 2014; Whiteman and Cooper, 2016). Finally, others have studied how BOP solutions disregard environmental impacts (Bendul et al., 2017; Gold et al., 2013).

Gutiérrez et al. (2016) identify how, when scaled up, BOP business models lose their cross-sectoral nature, privileging intra-sectoral partnerships and market mechanisms to coordinate transactions. Exploratory stages of IDNs require cross-sector partnerships with other entities for the company to take advantage of social capital, resources, and knowledge about BOP markets. However, by implementing the BOP model, the company absorbs its cross-sector partners' market knowledge, and devotes resources to strengthening intra-sectoral partnerships and increasing resource efficiency and control. Reffico and Gutiérrez (2016) illustrate the difficulties of reaching ambidexterity—the parallel coexistence of two different business models, a traditional BM and an IDN, within a single established MNC—using established capabilities while creating new combinations of resources for other business models (Hill and Birkinshaw, 2012, cited in Reffico and Gutiérrez, 2016, p. 464). Difficulties in reaching ambidexterity include: Obstacles to create coalitions for change, disparate interests between upper and middle levels, cost of capital, risk aversion, perceptions of paternalism towards the alternative BM, and reluctance to devote resources to this BM, allocating those resources, instead, to other more profitable projects (Reficco and Gutiérrez, 2016). While Gutiérrez et al. (2016) identify the use of intra-sectoral collaboration to achieve efficiencies, a gap remains regarding the internal mechanisms whereby MNCs can gain efficiencies leading to less cross-sectoral collaboration in the business model. These authors call for further research on the evolution and patterns of heterogeneous portfolios of firms venturing in the BOP segment, on studies with CSOs as anchor organisations for analysis, and other research connecting configuration patterns with performance outcomes. Reficco and Gutiérrez (2016) identify the obstacles organisations face in reaching ambidexterity. However, little is known at field level about the mechanisms that strengthen the inertias that thwart sustainability. Our work advances on these lines.

Crane et al. (2014) detect several deficiencies in shared value models, including IDNs. Shared value propositions tend to ignore the tension between economic and social goals within organisations. Instead of creating value for all stakeholders, companies tend to capture most of the value for themselves, while "systemic injustice has not been solved and the poverty of marginalised stakeholders might even have increased because of the engagement of the corporation" (Crane et al., 2014, p. 137). Upon facing the challenges that shared value models pose, companies use decoupling mechanisms. Decoupling, as described by Whiteman and Cooper (2016) and Crane et al. (2014), refers to an organisational practice in which companies forgo a line of work, when indicators and goals are perceived to have been reached—even if they have not—to allow the system to continue working (Meyer and Rowan, 1977). To decouple, institutions resort to: Announcing, yet not implementing, social programs; delegating tasks to other professionals in the field; avoiding integration of activities, for example, integrating separate environmental activities within a quality norm; "ceremonialising" inspections and evaluations through huge events to launch quality programs; allowing employees to work informally; and making goals ambiguous or flexible (Meyer and Rowan,1977, cited in Whiteman and Cooper, 2016, p. 119). Consequently, actors have to deal with incompatible demands and even tend to avoid their social responsibilities (Whiteman and Cooper, 2016).

Finally, Bendul et al. (2017) and Gold et al. (2013) state that BOP businesses have disregarded their ecological impact in favor of their main economic aim. Companies concentrate on social impact and on reducing costs to offer affordable products and services to BOP communities (Bendul et al., 2017), but the environmental costs of reaching those consumers and the lack of infrastructure available to disposed of consumed goods are seldom considered. This is why BOP businesses must reconsider their activities, integrating sustainability concepts into the supply chain, from production to responsible consumption (Gold et al., 2013). Companies focus on cost reduction and social development, even if this implies more waste, as ecological awareness among BOP market consumers seems to be very low (Bendul et al., 2017). In fact, some authors argue that tradeoffs are unavoidable and that a triple bottom line does not apply to BOP markets, but rather, a double line composed of social and economic performance (Gold et al., 2013; Hahn, 2009; Kandachar and Halme, 2007). Even if organisations try to impose environmental guidelines and policies, it is common to find disconnections in their implementation between traditional distribution channels and those of the BOP (Gold et al., 2013).

An additional challenge comes from the fact that most literature on IDNs uses empirical studies with only partial data. Data is collected at one point in time, usually during the start-up phase of the implementation, and for a very limited time span (Reficco and Gutiérrez, 2016). Our methodological approach, using data from the start-up and the scale-up phases, overcomes this limitation allowing us to respond to the research question: How do changes in IDNs scale-up business models affect the sustainability dimensions of the value proposition?

Case descriptions

This analysis focuses on five cases in five Latin American countries where MNCs implemented IDNs. Case 1 is the IDN of a food and beverage MNC that has operated in the Dominican Republic since 2006. The IDN was developed, in accordance with the MNC's corporate values, to reach isolated, low-income communities not served by traditional channels. Local authorised distributors sent combos of packaged food products, such as coffee, powdered cereal, and milk, to Level 1 (L1) micro-sellers. L1 micro-sellers motivated, monitored, and redistributed products to Level 2 (L2) micro-sellers, who sold the products on a door-to-door basis. Coordinators hired by the MNC recruited, monitored, and trained groups of 25 to 30 L1 micro-sellers. Training included topics such as entrepreneurship, nutrition, and life skills. Recruitment was mainly conducted through referrals. MNC supervisors controlled and monitored authorised distributors by geographic areas. The MNC formed a cross-sectoral alliance with a Non-Profit Organisation (NPO)[1], which had been providing financial services to the poor, as well as financial training and microcredits to L1 and L2 micro-sellers since 2012 (see Figure 4.1). Microcredits for L1 micro-sellers ranged from US $200 to US $330; L2 micro-sellers could access microcredits from US $45 to US $67 (see Figure 4.1).

CASE 1

Figure 4.1 IDN Case 1. Data retrieved: 2015, 2016. Source: Authors *Last set of available data from the mid-term evaluation.

Case 2 refers to an IDN developed through a private foundation's program that provides jobs to female heads of household and access to a portfolio of high-quality food, personal, and household care products, ranging from oatmeal, cookies, and tuna, to shampoo and laundry detergent to remote communities. The foundation created a social enterprise with the aim of developing local businesses to overcome poverty, while fostering the entrepreneurial capabilities of their owners. The IDN was the first project of the social enterprise and has been operating in rural Peru since 2013. MNC distributers and local firms sent products to the social enterprise, after which, delivery logistics adapted to two types of L2 micro-sellers. L2 Direct micro-sellers received products directly from the social enterprise. L2 Indirect micro-sellers received products through the intermediation of L1 micro-sellers. L1 micro-sellers also managed inventory, charged bills, and trained L2 Indirect micro-sellers. Some employees of the social enterprise, known as promoters, monitored and trained L1 micro-sellers and L2 Direct micro-sellers. The social enterprise established alliances with suppliers, NGOs, and governmental organisations for recruitment and hiring. Besides the rural operation, in 2016, the social enterprise launched an urban operation hub, which sold to middle- and high-income urban segments—which we refer to as TOP (Top of the Pyramid markets)—and supported some deliveries to low-income rural areas (see Figure 4.2). The managers expected this urban operation to cover the rural IDN's financial deficit, but it did not. The IDN did not meet its break-even point in the fourth quarter of 2016, and from March to October 2017, the IDN gradually closed its operations.

Case 3 is an IDN created in 2012 by an international NGO in Nicaragua. Its objective was to provide communities with high-quality nutritional products

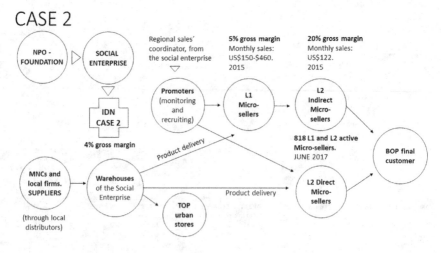

Figure 4.2 IDN Case 2. Data retrieved: 2015, 2017. Source: Authors *Last set of available data from the mid-term evaluation.

and to improve the living conditions of micro-sellers. The NGO held a micro-franchise and L1 micro-sellers usually ran the IDN3 stores from home. The stores' policy included high quality, low prices, and healthy products, such as eggs, cheese, chicken, and fruit. The NGO purchased them from several local suppliers and processed, repacked, and sent them on consignment to the L1 micro-sellers' stores. L1 micro-sellers were recruited by contacting churches, government organisations, or schools or through referrals. L1 micro-sellers filled out a demographics form and attended an interview, after which an NGO representative checked the store's conditions and helped to set it up. Once a week, the representative checked the inventory levels and made a preorder of the goods to be delivered to each store. The NGO offered L1 micro-sellers training in business and empowerment, as well as other benefits such as psychological and social support, life insurance, and school savings plans. The IDN3 did not involve alliances with financial institutions (see Figure 4.3).

Case 4 is that of dairy project MNC in Brazil, set up in partnership with an international and a local NGO that supported entrepreneurship. The IDN was created in 2011 as one of the MNC's alternative channels, in compliance with its CSR policy. Alternative distributors (not exclusive) delivered products such as yogurt, milk, and bottled water. As in Case 2, there were two types of L2 micro-sellers. L2 Direct micro-sellers received products directly from alternative distributors. L2 Indirect micro-sellers received products through the intermediation of L1 micro-sellers. L1 also recruited and trained L2 Indirect micro-sellers, who then sold the products on a door-to-door basis. After receiving the orders, L1 and L2 micro-sellers had 28 days to pay for them. Three categories of L2 micro-sellers were set up to help differentiate their incentives and payment terms, according to monthly sales. The MNC managed the IDN and recruited

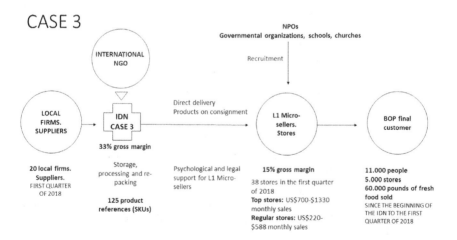

Figure 4.3 IDN Case 3. Data retrieved: first quarter of 2018. Source: Authors

CASE 4

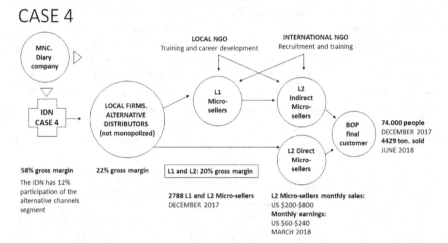

Figure 4.4 IDN Case 4. Data retrieved: 2017, 2018. Source: Authors *Last set of available data from the mid-term evaluation.

micro-sellers with some support from the international NGO. L2 micro-sellers were recruited mainly through referrals, and authorised distributors sometimes helped out in recruiting L2 micro-sellers. Distributors found it cheaper to send products directly to the L2 micro-sellers, which saved paying commissions to L1 micro-sellers. The local NGO provided technical assistance and virtual training to micro-sellers and authorised distributors. The IDN did not involve alliances with financial institutions (see Figure 4.4).

Case 5 is that of an IDN developed by a social enterprise, the result of a joint venture between a local food and beverage company and an NPO (Global Risk Fund), in Costa Rica. The company distributed combinations of fortified, powdered soup, juice, cereal, and beverage mixes through retailers (convenience stores, supermarkets), institutional channels (schools, hospitals, and governmental programs), and the IDN. The IDN value proposition was to become the main source of income for female heads of household and was aimed at decreasing malnutrition levels in poor, urban communities. The company delivered products to L1 micro-sellers and L2 micro-sellers. Some L1 micro-sellers were in charge of L2 micro-sellers, sent them products, and paid commissions for their final sales. Most L1 micro-sellers, however, sold the products on a door-to-door basis, directly to final customers to earn greater margins. Once the orders were placed, L1 and L2 micro-sellers had two weeks to pay back the cost of advancing the products. Training was run by the company, while a regional NGO (a Latin American financial institution) and a global NGO (microfinance institution) recruited, provided microcredits, and supported recruitment activities (see Figure 4.5).

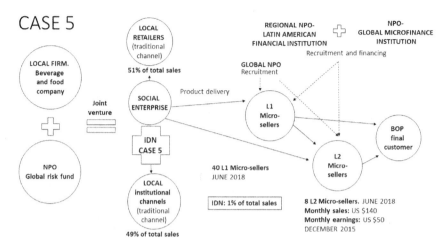

Figure 4.5 IDN Case 5. Data retrieved: 2015, 2018. Source: Authors *Last set of available data from the mid-term evaluation.

Methods

We conducted midterm evaluations of the scale-up process in five IDNs to assess: (a) The relevance of the IDN to the country context where it operated; (b) qualitative and quantitative results related to the structuring of the IDN, number of beneficiaries, execution of activities, budget execution, and impact of the IDN on micro-sellers; and (c) processes and implementation of the IDN. Table 4.1 depicts relevant data about the cases.

We did a desk review of administrative and operational reports, secondary data provided by the multilateral fund that supplied seed capital for the IDNs' scale-up, and at least two working papers by academics of the Social Enterprise Knowledge Network (SEKN) that analysed the cases' processes. Our data collection included two field visits for each case where L1 and L2 micro-sellers, representatives of the anchor organisation (i.e., social enterprise, MNC, NGO), distributors, and suppliers participated in interviews and focus groups. In total, we had 77 participants in individual interviews and 10 focus groups with an average of 4 to 6 participants each.

For data analysis, we analysed verbatim transcriptions of all interviews and focus groups. First, we did this within case content analysis, identifying interest-ing themes that emerged from the data. Second, we did cross-case analysis, iden-tifying common and divergent patterns in the five cases. At this point, we shared our preliminary findings with representatives of anchor organisations and the funding organisation, and we received feedback and alternative interpretations that complemented ours. With this clarity about commonalities and divergences

Table 4.1 Characterization of the studied cases

Case	Place	Anchor organisation	Products	Start-up date	Scaled-up date	Assessment date (Data collection)	Contribution from the executing organisation	Contribution from the multilateral fund	Total investment (USD)
1	Dominican Republic	Multinational Company	Food and beverages	2006	2016	August 2017	US$650,000 (62%)	US$ 400,000 (38%)	US$1,050,000
2	Peru	Social Enterprise	Food, personal, and household care products	2013	2017	November 2017	US$1,000,000 (33%)	US$ 500,000 (33%)	US$1,500,000
3	Nicaragua	NGO	Food and beverages	2012	2017	February 2018	US$412,000 (51%)	US$ 400,000 (49%)	US$ 812,000
4	Brazil	Multinational Company	Dairy	2011	2016	June 2018	US$1,270,500 (61%)	US$ 800,000 (39%)	US$2,070,500
5	Costa Rica	Social Enterprise	Powdered food and beverages	2013	2018	June 2018	US$418,500 (51%)	US$ 400,000 (49%)	US$818,500
TOTAL							US$3,751,000	US$2,500,000	US$6,251,000

Note. Data from agreements and terms of reference of each case.

across cases in the evolution of their business models, we moved to the next step. Third, we drafted analytical memos about the changes to the business model in each case, which served as the primary basis for the preparation of a comparative chart of start-up and scaled-up business models. The analytical memos and charts helped us to identify changes in the IDNs' start-up and scale-up business models and their effects on the sustainability dimensions of the value proposition. Finally, we exploited the differences in the sample to compare the evolution of cross-sector partnerships where the anchor organisation was an MNC (Cases 1 and 4) with those where the anchor was an NGO (Case 3) or a social enterprise (Cases 2 and 5).

Results: IDNs' Business Model changes reinforcing distribution inertias that thwart sustainability

All the IDNs studied ran pilot projects before the scale-up. During their start-up, all the cases used business models that contained multiple flexible and sometimes paternalistic elements that facilitated good results in most of the pilot projects. All five cases had to make several adjustments for the scale-up, affecting dimensions like distribution costs, route planning, use of Information and Communications Technology (ICTs), inventory management, and financial sustainability. Table 4.2 illustrates the major differences in those elements in the start-up versus the scaled-up business models in the five cases.

The adjusted, scaled-up, business models responded to the need of anchor organisations' to meet a break-even point as a key prerequisite for taking the models to scale. These adjustments, however, strengthened the inertias of the distribution field such as reinforcing the power and status of traditional distributors and firms' dependencies with these distributors; reinforcing social exclusion; maintaining last-mile constraints; privileging non-nutritive, high-turnover foods in the product mix portfolios; reducing flexibility for micro-sellers imposing strict controls on their time and movements without formalising their labor; and concentrating control of the anchor organisations in the organisational ecosystem. All of these inertias thwarted the elements of sustainability that had been included in the start-up business models, resulting in IDNs operating as "business as usual" Table 4.3 identifies the main changes in the business models, the inertias these changes reinforced, and their effects on sustainability dimensions.

To reduce high distribution costs, MNCs, NGOs, and social enterprises used different strategies that helped them improve delivery timing and precision. At the outset, IDN1 deliveries were made by the MNC, but later the MNC formed an alliance with authorised distributors that did same-day deliveries. This strategy allowed the MNC to reach a higher number of micro-sellers, optimise costs, focus on its core business, and scale-up the model. The MNC on IDN4 developed a whole network of alternative distributors that solved delivery logistics. This was possible thanks to market conditions, given that distributors in Brazil had no sole control over certain areas, as is the case in other Latin

Table 4.2 Major business model adjustments in scaled-up IDNs

Case	IDN BM dimension	Start-up BM	Scaled-up BM
1	Distribution cost	• MNC distributors sent combos of products to L1 micro-sellers, who were responsible for delivering products and monitoring L2 micro-sellers. • As distributors simultaneously served other channels of the MNC, delays were frequent and distribution costs were high for the MNC. • Monitoring, support, and motivation of L1 micro-sellers was difficult.	• MNCs created an additional level of coordinators who were experienced micro-sellers and monitored groups of 25–30 L1 micro-sellers. They also supported and motivated micro-sellers. As a result, retention rates improved. • MNCs outsourced distribution and gave exclusivity to distributors. There was one supervisor per authorised distributor.
	Route planning	• The MNC managed distribution logistics, which was time consuming and did not allow the MNC to focus on its core operations.	• Local authorised distributors sent products directly to L1 micro-sellers, according to route plans.
	Use of ICTs	• Monitoring and control technologies were not bold enough to capture data for L2 micro-sellers and conduct rigorous follow-up. • L1 micro-sellers explained benefits to consumers.	• Along with the MNC, the NPO developed a new ICT to track sales of the L1 and L2 micro-sellers, but disagreements about ownership appeared and the process to develop the app stopped.
	Inventory management	The MNC, as a producer, controlled costs and inventory levels. The MNC leveraged its reputation to access BOP markets.	Frequent change of portfolio composition affected consumers. Also, nutritional value posed a risk for them.
	Financial sustainability	• Some L1 micro-sellers did not pay for products because they thought the IDN was a philanthropy program. The MNC experienced losses. • Retention rate was 1–3%, because L1 micro-sellers had access to other sources of income (such as subsidies). • The MNC granted loans but faced high default rates given its lack of experience in this area. • The MNC provided training in life skills, nutrition, and entrepreneurship.	• Break-even point was met later than expected, but the IDN was sustained by income from other channels of the MNC. • An allied NPO granted loans and provided training. This reduced default rates and allowed the MNC to focus on its core business. • Loans were insufficient to buy varied and complete portfolios, leading to slow adoption. • Alliances with distributors improved deliveries and reduced costs for the MNC.

(*Continued*)

Table 4.2 Continued

Case	IDN BM dimension	Start-up BM	Scaled-up BM
2	Distribution cost	• The Social Enterprise (SE*) bought food, personal, and household care products from distributors (not directly from producers) and stored them in warehouses, where L1 micro-sellers could pick them up. L1 micro-sellers sold the products door-to-door in rural areas. • The SE trained L1-micro-sellers in basic business and leadership skills.	• New distributors sent products to the SE. L1 and L2 Direct micro-sellers received products from the SE. L2 Indirect micro-sellers received products from L1 micro-sellers. • Supervisors monitored and trained L1 micro-sellers and L2 Direct micro-sellers. L1 micro-sellers managed inventory and trained L2 Indirect micro-sellers.
	Route planning	• L1 micro-sellers walked long distances, carrying heavy weights of products, in order to earn minimum sales quotas.	• Besides door-to-door sales, L1 and L2 micro-sellers began to sell at fairs and rural markets. This cannibalised the sales of some suppliers who later left the IDN.
	Use of ICTs	• The SE tracked activity from a regional supervisor, but it did not have information about L1-micro-sellers.	• The SE did not have up-to-date information about L1–L2 micro-sellers. Information was hardly scaling up.
	Inventory management	• L1 micro-sellers received products on consignment. They had one month to pay or to return products. However, the SE experienced losses due to the bad condition of returned products. There were no alliances between distributors and the SE, making distributors' permanence, inventory availability, and prices uncertain. This fact undermined consumers' confidence.	• Only cash payment was allowed. • Offers were unstable, given the lack of alliances with new distributors. New brands weren´t recognised in rural areas, or products did not fit rural needs (e.g., the portfolio included floor wax, but houses had cement or clay floors). Previously, L1 and L2 micro-sellers advised some portfolio changes that were not executed.

(Continued)

Table 4.2 Continued

Case	IDN BM dimension	Start-up BM	Scaled-up BM
	Financial sustainability	• A pilot was run at the IDN planning stage (2014). Distributors stated up to 40% price discounts, but at the start-up they gave discounts of 7%. The SE gave up on its margins to protect L1–L2 micro-sellers' margins. • The SE did not establish alliances with financial entities or NPOs, claiming this strategy prevented micro-sellers from acquiring loans they couldn't pay later.	• New distributors did not sign alliances with the SE. This led to unstable prices and low margins for the SE, which was still fighting to protect margins of L1 and L2 micro-sellers. • The SE launched an urban operation hub to cover the IDN financial deficit, but it did not. The IDN did not meet its break-even point, and the IDN gradually closed its operations.
3	Distribution cost	• Local suppliers sent ingredients and semi-processed products to the NGO, which stored, processed and repacked them. The NGO sent final products to the stores of L1 micro-sellers. Their stores opened at least 8 hours per day. • The NGO recruited L1 micro-sellers.	• Distribution followed the same procedures as at the start-up stage. A representative from the NGO checked good store conditions and helped to set up the store. • Allied governmental organisations, schools, and churches recruited micro-sellers.
	Route planning	• The NGO had the whole list of stores, time for pre-sales in each store, and transportation times on a single route.	• Route planning was improved thanks to Operations Management Analysis.
	Use of ICTs	• The NGO controlled the inventory for each store through tailored software. However, recording sales relied on L1 micro-sellers' honesty and skills, which is why they were trained in technical issues, finances, and personal well-being.	• The software was improved to optimise routes. • Training was broadened to cover topics such as psychological and legal advisory.

(*Continued*)

Table 4.2 Continued

Case	IDN BM dimension	Start-up BM	Scaled-up BM
	Inventory management	• A representative of the NGO took weekly orders at each store. Products were delivered on consignment, according to sales average and history of payment. Representatives also responded to doubts and clarified accounts. • The NGO had a restrictive policy of offering only affordable, healthy products. But customers still asked for unhealthy products.	• Weekly supply remained the same as at the start-up stage. • The NGO added 90 healthy products to the portfolio. It reached 115 SKUs by 2017, in comparison to 2000 SKUs in traditional stores. • Audit activities became more rigorous, to secure stores' management codes.
	Financial sustainability	• Alliances with suppliers secured margins and product availability. • Retention rates were as high as 84%. • L1 micro-sellers signed a guarantee deposit as back-up in case of closing stores with debts.	• Alliances with suppliers remained. • Sales of healthy products only, long working hours, and difficulties meeting accounting practices reduced the retention rate to 25%.
4	Distribution cost	• The IDN belonged to a network of non-traditional channels of the MNC. The MNC delivered combos of products to alternative distributors (neither monopolised or exclusive). They sent products to L1 micro-sellers, who, in turn, delivered products to L2 micro-sellers. • Sometimes the distributors trained and recruited L1 and L2 micro-sellers. • L1 micro-sellers recruited, trained, motivated, and lent money to L2 micro-sellers, who sold the products door-to-door.	• Distribution logistics remained the same as at the start-up stage. • Distributors preferred to avoid sales commissions paid to L1 micro-sellers. They began to sell directly to some L2 micro-sellers. As a result, 60% L2 micro-sellers were not supervised by an L1 micro-seller. • L2 micro-sellers were categorised at three levels, according to their sales levels. According to their category they received prizes and other benefits.
	Route planning	• Route planning was developed through market research.	• Route planning continued to be optimised.

(*Continued*)

Table 4.2 Continued

Case	IDN BM dimension	Start-up BM	Scaled-up BM
	Use of ICTs	• An allied local NGO provided recruiting, technical assistance, and virtual training to distributors and L1–L2 micro-sellers. • There were disagreements because the MNC expected fast financial results, and the NGO looked for integral outcomes in the long term.	• Organic growth of the IDN reduced the relevance of the NGO for recruitment strategies. • Distributors sent statistics to the MNC, but there was no additional audit process. • Disagreements remained.
	Inventory management	• Combos of products were developed through a market research study. • The MNC controlled production and inventory availability.	• Combos evolved according to the growth of the IDN. • Production and inventory levels were still controlled by the MNC.
	Financial sustainability	• The MNC, as producer, had control of its own costs and inventory levels. Also, it had other distribution channels to support sales of this IDN, if required. • As alternative distributors had their own working capital, the MNC reduced its risk and focused on its core operation.	• By March of 2018, the IDN had met its break-even point. • The IDN allowed the MNC to accomplish its objectives of Social Responsibility. • L1 and L2 micro-sellers were in a process of job formalisation and the MNC was developing alliances to offer them loans.
5	Distribution cost	• The IDN was the alternative distribution channel of the SE. The IDN also sold beverages from an allied company. • The SE sent products to L1 and L2 micro-sellers. They sold the products in their communities.	• L1 micro-sellers perceived a high risk of backing up sales of L2 micro-sellers. Thus, L1 micro-sellers made direct sales to final consumers instead of delivering products to L2 micro-sellers.
	Route planning	• As the IDN was one of the several distribution channels—among convenience stores and supermarkets—the company was aware of the risk of cannibalisation and established lower prices for the IDN channel. • One truck attended the whole urban area.	• Route planning remained the same as in the start-up stage, as long as executives disagreed on the relevance and capability to attend rural markets.

(Continued)

Table 4.2 Continued

Case	IDN BM dimension	Start-up BM	Scaled-up BM
	Use of ICTs	• Both a regional and a global NPO trained L1 and L2 micro-sellers in technical issues. • The SE trained L1–L2 micro-sellers in soft skills and entrepreneurship. • There was no ICT to monitor the IDN.	• The SE hired a consultancy to create a base line of the IDN and to improve technology tools and training procedures. • The SE was developing an app for L1–L2 micro-sellers to place orders.
	Inventory management	• Products were sold under a credit format: L1 and L2 micro-sellers received products and they had up to two weeks to pay. To place new orders L1–L2 micro-sellers had to be up to date with payments.	• Products continued to be sold under credit format. • Product combos and sales on demand to institutional customers were executed. • There was disagreement between healthy and traditional products in the portfolio.
	Financial sustainability	• The SE captured margin value controlling its own production. • L1 and L2 micro-sellers' average sales quotas were lower than expected, because they were working 3–4 hours per day, 5 days a week, in comparison to the expected 8 hours per day. • Training costs were very high.	• The SE expected to increase participation of the allied beverage company, reducing some control over margins. • Break-even point was far from being met, due to a small group of L1–L2 micro-sellers achieving minimum sales' quotas. • To reduce costs, training was shortened to 2 days and directed by the SE.

*In the tables, we use SE for Social Enterprise.

American countries. Networks created by an NGO or a social enterprise as an anchor organisation did not own enough distribution channels, nor did they have enough bargaining power with distributors, preventing cost reduction and logistics optimisation. The NGO of IDN3 distributed products directly, but since it did not own production, it could only optimise routing and delivery costs through weekly orders.

A distribution cost-reduction strategy, adopted by IDN1, IDN2, IDN4, and IDN5, was to rearrange micro-sellers into two distinct levels: L1 micro-sellers who placed orders and redistributed products to L2 micro-sellers. This resulted in fewer points of delivery and lower distribution costs. A leader of IDN5 remembered:

Table 4.3 BMs' adjustments, reinforced distribution field inertias, effects on sustainability

IDN BM adjustment (mechanism that reinforces)	Reinforced inertias in the distribution field	Effects on sustainability value dimensions
Distribution costs Reducing operational costs and improving delivery timing and precision by establishing alliances between MNCs and traditional distributors or establishing new network of alternative distributors (IDN4). NGOs/SEs do not have alternative distribution channels or negotiation power with traditional distributors. MNCs/NGOs/SEs rearrange micro-sellers into two distinct levels: micro-sellers (L1) and micro-sellers (L2).	Maintains the status quo reinforcing traditional distributors' power and firms' dependency on these distributors. Creates a structure of intermediation where better-trained, more experienced women (L1) coordinate ones that are more vulnerable (L2),reinforcing social exclusion. Maintains the order of discounts in direct sales. Maintains last-mile constraints (reinforcing exclusion from those areas).	Economic efficiency. Cannot reduce costs or optimise logistics. Economic efficiency. Economic value capture for women in L1 became higher and more concentrated when compared to value captured by women in the L2 level (Mostly self-consumption. IDN becomes a way to promote consumption patterns to gain status instead of a mechanism to resolve poverty). High levels of control over women's time and activities without work formalisation, and constraining their entrepreneurial spirit.
Route planning MNCs and NGOs establish sales routes for micro-sellers, avoiding overlapping with traditional distributors and market cannibalisation. Concentration of routes in zones with high population density.	Reinforces traditional distributors' power and dependencies. Reduces flexibility of the IDN for micro-sellers without labor formalisation. Reinforcement of last-mile constrains. In the rural areas high fragmentation and operational costs made the model non-feasible.	Micro-sellers found other competitors in areas assigned to them and had to work harder to comply with sales targets. The IDN was not serving BOP markets in last-mile areas.

(Continued)

Table 4.3 Continued

IDN BM adjustment (mechanism that reinforces)	Reinforced inertias in the distribution field	Effects on sustainability value dimensions
Use of ICTs Coordination of actors in the organisational ecosystem of the IDN. Control and monitoring of sales and micro-sellers' progress. To develop market intelligence, taking advantage of micro-sellers' closeness to the final consumer.	Reinforces control of the anchor organisation in the whole system allowing them to stop working with some of those micro-credit institutions. Some NGOs supporting the program. Refines financial models to improve IDNs' management, increasing control of micro-sellers' use of time without labor formalisation. Micro-sellers' closeness to final consumers facilitated to launch new products. Micro-sellers assuming the risk for these new products while traditional distributors do not take that risk. They prefer high-turnover products.	The organisational ecosystem is cross-sectoral while the companies learn how to conduct the business. Cross-sectorality is lost once the scale-up is achieved. Women lose flexibility without gaining labor formalisation. Micro-sellers buffer MNCs and big NGOs risk for launching new products or low-turnover products.
Inventory management To reduce inventory loss and default rates, companies changed product mix in the micro-sellers' portfolios (adding unhealthy products). Companies eliminated consigned products.	Companies privilege traditional products (high turnover, low prices) instead of healthy ones or the ones preferred by clients, or they push new products or products not sold through other channels into the IDN. Only high-rotation products are sold.	Customers and L2 micro-sellers had access to traditional products (sugary, sodas, expensive shampoo, and cleaning products). Trust between micro-seller and communities affected by not maintaining a stable portfolio of products. Micro-sellers absorb the risk for unsold products.

(Continued)

Table 4.3 Continued

IDN BM adjustment (mechanism that reinforces)	Reinforced inertias in the distribution field	Effects on sustainability value dimensions
Financial sustainability In the scale-up, as financial aid diminishes, anchor organisations made adjustments to reach financial sustainability. IDNs achieved break-even points in times longer than expected by MNCs, NGOs, and SEs. IDNs labor-intensiveness makes economies of scale harder to reach.	Search for economic efficiencies, which is the dominant logic in the distribution business. The pressure to meet break-even points ends up with scaled-up business model without consideration of social or environmental dimensions. Profits below anchor organisations' expectations. Economies of scale hard to achieve. IDN became "boutique" initiatives within the organisations.	Return to a "business as usual" model that did not pay enough attention to social and environmental aspects of the IDN original value proposition. Despite small positive social impacts and negative environmental externalities, anchor organisations continued to advertise IDNs in their sustainability reports.

We were efficient recruiting but inefficient at monitoring. Why? Because the supervisor of 400 micro-sellers was the CEO of the social enterprise. Among the commercial operation, products' development, service to the micro-sellers, and monitoring were not optimum. Therefore, it becomes useful to have two levels of micro-sellers.

Sometimes, L1 micro-sellers were located in dangerous or distant areas, and their sales were so low (up to USD $80, monthly), that companies opted for reducing the frequency or stopping deliveries altogether, leaving products at other locations for pick up. The addition of this new L1 micro-seller level had several implications for the value proposition, which we will discuss in depth hereinafter.

These changes to optimise distribution costs, and logistics reinforced the power of traditional distributors in the value chain, maintaining the levels of dependency between anchor organisations and distributors. They also created a structure of intermediation where better-trained, more experienced L1-level women coordinated more vulnerable L2-level women, reinforcing social exclusion by preventing the most vulnerable women from earning higher incomes. The pyramidal structure among anchor organisation coordinators, L1, and L2 women maintained the order of discounts used in direct sales. Finally, the optimisation of the logistics maintained the well-known constraints of last-mile distribution, reinforcing social and economic exclusion in those areas.

Anchor organisations made other adjustments to strengthen the inclusive distribution channel, giving access to credit, but working capital suffered and default rates became difficult to control. In addition, the attention that should have been devoted to the IDNs' main activities was diverted, as remembered by one employee in the anchor company of IDN1:

> We did not have the required technical capabilities to develop a micro-credit functional area. The company's core always had been commercialisation of products of high rotation but not microfinancing activities. Based on a growth prospect, the Multinational Company financed the working capital of micro-sellers, which dramatically increased default rates.

Partnerships with NPOs providing financial services were initially deemed as crucial to sustainability and scalability, as they allowed micro-sellers to buy and sell greater volumes and to create an impact throughout the chain. But microcredits were directed to education and inventory and house purchases. Micro-sellers were encouraged to achieve personal savings goals. At best, they managed to buy aspirational products (houses, cars, appliances). Another benefit for women in the channel was their access to comprehensive, high-quality training provided by anchor organisations. They offered training in areas such as health, nutrition, finances, and life and business skills. In some contexts, they offered more specific training: In IDN2, micro-sellers received some training on domestic violence, while IDN1's company trained micro-sellers in which locations were safe to sell in.

Route planning and reinforced inertias

Anchor organisations, in collaboration with distributors, established the sales routes (the route trajectories women should follow to do their sales) for micro-sellers. The NGO of IDN3 managed presale schedules for all stores, including transportation schedules. The company in IDN5 optimised the assignment of micro-sellers per geographical area to prevent overlapping of sales points and customers. Besides route planning, some companies allowed micro-sellers to operate in other places: For example, IDN2's social enterprise allowed L1 and L2 micro-sellers to sell at fairs, rural markets, and peripheral areas. This strategy had questionable results because it cannibalised the market and created serious problems with traditional distributors, who left IDN2. Routing plans also had to consider the micro-sellers' safety. Aware of this, the MNC of IDN1 promoted secure routes and informed micro-sellers of the most dangerous areas they should avoid. IDN3 operated in a complex area, leading micro-sellers to demand secure payment methods, instead of cash. A final aspect to which companies paid little attention was that, with the optimisation of routes, micro-sellers had to walk long distances for long periods in order to meet their sales quota. Even though IDNs claimed to be flexible models, the fact was that micro-sellers had to devote most of their time to this job if they wanted to achieve the monthly income that IDNs proposed. One participant in IDN2 recalled "these women have several occupations—childcare, animal husbandry, farming—so they have very little time left for sales. This fact was belittled at the pilot stage."

Another challenge found by micro-sellers in the execution of sales routes was the high density of competitors, especially in urban areas. Our sample showed that an IDN's success´ depended on high population density. IDNs operating in rural areas, like IDN2, found high fragmentation and operational costs that made the model non-feasible; IDN5 considered rural expansion but could not find distributors to serve those areas. But high density was no panacea: Operation in high-density areas led, in some cases, to market cannibalisation, as explained earlier. But IDNs who targeted remote areas, assuming that branded products were not available there, found that market coverage in remote areas was very wide (as in IDN2), even for recognised brands.

Changes in route planning also reinforced traditional distributors' power and anchor organisations' dependencies on these actors. They also increased the time micro-sellers devoted to this task, but their efforts were not matched by labor formalisation. Again, the optimisation of routes following economic criteria reinforced last-mile constraints and social exclusion.

Use of Information and Communication Technologies and reinforced inertias

Another element required for the successful scale-up of BMs was the use of Information and Communications Technologies (ICT). ICT and sales technology were crucial to coordination among actors in the network, control and monitoring of sales and the progress of micro-sellers, and feeding market intelligence. High-quality data and adequate and timely flux of information enabled the generation of more refined financial models to improve the management of IDNs.

IDNs, however, showed various weaknesses in this regard. The MNC and NGO of IDN1, for example, managed information almost manually, with some data entered into an Excel spreadsheet. They developed a system to coordinate micro-sellers, but once it was developed, the organisations disagreed on data property since it was the MNC's information but used on a platform developed by the NPO, based on its experience and capabilities. For IDN3, executives expected a bold technological tool for inventory management, which turned out to be too big for such a small operation. For IDN4, distributors retrieved the micro-sellers' billing information and sent it to the MNC, which did not have proper auditing mechanisms for this channel. Distributors were SMEs without much capacity; they communicated with micro-sellers' via telephone and WhatsApp. IDN3 installed 70 computers for cash management, but due to high desertion rates, computers were lost. IDN5 was developing an app for micro-sellers to place orders, but it was not ready for identity verification. IDN2 showed fluctuations of information and coordination that did not work horizontally or vertically. In general, ICTs required an evolution to fulfill the purpose of effectively implementing sales technology and improving the monitoring and control of the micro-sellers' activities.

Another crucial function of ICTs was to support new market opportunities that came from micro-sellers' closeness to customers. Studied IDNs increased their knowledge on BOP markets as a result of micro-sellers' closeness to and recognition of final customers. This knowledge became valuable when it escalated from the network's lower to upper levels and materialised in the strategic planning, which was facilitated by ICTs. This knowledge transfer not always happens: Sometimes micro-sellers transmitted this information to their supervisors, who could not escalate to the next level of management, or, if the supervisors transmitted the information, upper-level management did not take it seriously or had other priorities. One micro-seller in IDN2 stated: "I think they didn't see reality in the same way as we did. They were on one planet while we were on another one [...] we lacked communication with the supervisor."

Micro-sellers were successful brand ambassadors. They had social capital and legitimacy within their community. We found a strong association between confident female micro-sellers and the establishment of new commercial relationships. Micro-sellers also explained product benefits to customers and promoted new products' credibility trials based on their own experience and technical training. Most of the time, they did this with a high sense of belonging and affection for the brand. IDN1 executives claimed that the network was successful in launching new products, especially among customers hard to reach through mass advertising. At scale-up, IDN2 also attained the acceptance of some not-so-well-known products. Micro-sellers adapted offers to specific customer preferences (extra products or product combos). Companies supported micro-sellers with advertising, while small companies usually did this by means of external donations.

Even though the use of ICTs was far from ideal, the introduction and refinement of their use contributed to reinforcing inertias in the distribution field. Having more and better information flows reinforced control of the anchor organisation over the rest of the distribution chain, allowing anchors to stop working with some actors (e.g., micro-credit institutions and NGOs supporting the programs). Also, with the use of ICTs, some anchor organisations refined their financial models and management systems increasing control over micro-sellers' time without increasing labor formalisation. Using ICTs for marketing new products created situations where micro-sellers buffered the risk of launching these new products through other traditional channels, which preferred well-known, high-turnover products.

How inertias reinforced by changes in distribution cost, route planning, and ICTs thwarted sustainability

The changes made to business models aimed at controlling distribution costs, rearranging women in L1 and L2 levels, route planning, and the use of ICTs, lead to a reinforcement of the inertias of the distribution field. These changes affected the economic value created for the companies and the micro-sellers, the social value created for the micro-sellers, and the interaction value created through collaboration of the organisations in the ecosystem.

The effect of inertias on economic value creation

The economic value created for the anchor organisations increased with changes, in particular for MNCs. To the extent that such adjustments were made, anchor MNCs could stabilise a network role (not necessarily with the same women, since turnover was very high), increasing sales and profits. For instance, IDN1 sales after scaling up represented 2% of total national sales (from zero in previous years); IDN4 sold US $4.1 million in 2018, which represented about 2% of the national sales for the company with a net profit for the MNC of US $1.7 million. Both IDNs showed a positive growth trend, similar to those of other MNCs' distribution channels.

Unfortunately, while the economic value creation for companies improved, reinforcement of those inertias had negative effects on business models' sustainability dimensions related to women's wellbeing and the inclusiveness of the network. A key element of the IDNs value proposition was the creation of sustainable value for vulnerable women at the BOP. The main benefits for women identified in the evaluations were related to income, access to funding, training and technical support from companies, and psychological benefits such as a sense of belonging. All five IDNs became an alternative source of income, positively valued by L1 and L2 micro-sellers. Income from IDNs 2 and 5, however, was lower than each country's monthly minimum wage and the wage received from informal, alternative activities such as housekeeping or child care—for L2 micro-sellers and even for some L1 micro-sellers. As for IDN3, just 14 of its stores (6% of the stores run by L1 micro-sellers) reached incomes close to the alternative income or the minimum wage, about US $105–200, compared to an alternative income or minimum wage of US $175. Conversely, some L1 and L2 micro-sellers from IDN4 earned somewhat more than the minimum wage (US $240, compared to a minimum wage of US $231). Star L1 micro-sellers in IDN1 earned US $585–632, monthly, L1 micro-sellers earned US $175–233, and L2 micro-sellers, more than US $233, compared to an alternative income of US $164. Their income was also close to a monthly minimum wage of US $166–272.

In IDN1, L1 Star micro-sellers represented just 10% of L1 micro-sellers and had 50% of the L2 micro-sellers under their charge. Each L1 Star micro-seller received a monthly income of US $585–632, versus the L1 micro-sellers' average monthly income of US $175–233. Meanwhile, experienced L2 micro-sellers earned in ranges of US $585–1054, and new L2 micro-sellers earned US $ 233–291. IDN3 showed the same trend. TOP stores, which represented just 6%, had a monthly income of US $105–200, versus US $33–88 of average stores.

For the anchor organisations of IDN1, IDN2, IDN4, and IDN5, a key transition was responding to their limitations for accompanying, motivating, and supervising large numbers of L1 micro-sellers. This led anchor organisations to employ supervisors and to rearrange micro-sellers in the two levels. L1 micro-sellers accompanied, monitored, trained, and sometimes recruited L2 micro-sellers. This testimony illustrates some dynamics between them:

> The micro-seller is 50 years old and has 4 years of experience as a L1 micro-seller and 1 year of experience as a L2 micro-seller. She lends her credit card to 16 trustworthy L2 micro-sellers, so they can pay for products. Afterward, they pay her in cash.

For IDN3, only L1 micro-sellers participated. The two-level model sought to expedite L2 micro-sellers' management and distribution logistics and increase the total amount of micro-sellers and their sales.

The existence of a new micro-seller level changed the coordination and control system, creating problematic outcomes. First, the anchor organisation lost direct contact with and information about L2 micro-sellers. In most evaluations, women's progress was difficult to trace. Second, formalisation was uncertain. For example, IDN3 and IDN5 expected micro-sellers to work eight hours per day without a contract, a condition that could be typified as precarious and poor-quality employment. Third, we found a control paradox, whereby IDNs that claimed to develop micro-sellers' entrepreneurial spirit actually employed high levels of control that restricted entrepreneurship and did not consider the risks these women took. Finally, the most successful micro-sellers faced tax status problems. One of the oldest and most successful micro-sellers in IDN4 was detected by the country's tax system and was called in to account for unpaid taxes. She experienced serious cash problems while the company adjusted her tax status in the billing system.

L1 micro-sellers' time constraints and lack of incentives affected their role in recruiting, training, monitoring, and accompanying L2 micro-sellers. L1 micro-sellers usually had experience; they combined their work for the IDN with other direct sales projects and thus devoted little time to managing L2 micro-sellers. Some distributors preferred to work directly with L2 micro-sellers to avoid paying commissions to L1 micro-sellers.

The most significant consequence of these changes was the IDNs' transformation into purely market-based models. IDN chose experienced micro-sellers with superior commercial profiles over historically excluded BOP women. By solely focusing on economic value imposed by the capacity of IDNs to address the distributive justice, market failure was thwarted. Only L2 micro-sellers with outstanding commercial skills or externally experienced educated professionals were selected or promoted to the L1 level. Recruitment shifted from being inclusive and open to BOP women to focusing on micro-sellers with more professional profiles. Women with experience and sales skills—who had other work opportunities—were favored over the vulnerable BOP women. In the case of IDN3, where commercial skills or start-up capital was required from micro-sellers, allowing for women lacking basic sales skills to operate the stores, stores were shut down due to poor performance.

In terms of earnings, only some L1 micro-sellers with sharper professional profiles or commercial skills reached a significant income, while L2 micro-sellers only experienced a marginal shift in their income (see Income Pyramids in Appendix 1). In many cases, earnings amounted to women's own consumption of the products sold through the IDN.

The most common cause of desertion in all IDNs was the difficulty experienced by LW@ micro-sellers' in reaching the minimum sales required or at least earning the same amount as that of their alternative income. To achieve a decent income from selling mass consumption products, micro-sellers had to sell high volumes of products, which was aggravated by having to walk long distances in order to cover large geographical areas. Other micro-sellers left the program due to personal problems (death of relatives, care of children or elderly relatives, and family conflicts) and lack of compliance with IDNs' policies. One of the promises of the value proposition for women was the possibility of generating income with a flexible schedule and working from home so they could care for their children; however, as the BMs evolved, this part of the promise also became elusive.

Low retention of 3% to 10%, with a trend to decrease as the IDN went from the start-up to the scale-up phase, was a concern of all IDNs, as illustrated in this testimony: "many micro-sellers entered the IDN for potential sales, but when they realised how difficult door-to-door selling was and experienced low sales margins, they deserted." IDN1 experienced retention rates of 1% to 3%. IDN3 had a 10% retention rate, but only 1.75% of stores reached the expected performance. In IDN5, just 4 micro-sellers (10%), of which two were institutional actors, remained for the expansion stage. The program was left with just two individual micro-sellers, a 5% retention rate. Though we did not have any differentiated data between L1 and L2 micro-sellers available, it was possible to infer that retention rates were much lower and desertion much higher for L2 micro-sellers than for L1 micro-sellers, due to their lack of skills, low education levels, familiar constraints, heightened poverty and vulnerability, fewer benefits, and weaker communication with anchor organisations.

In IDN1, L1 micro-sellers experienced a significant income increase (US \$585–632 of Star L1 vs US \$175–233 of the average L1). These Star micro-sellers had a retention rate of 90%, but they amounted to just a few and were not necessarily vulnerable women at the BOP. On the other hand, most women in this network (97% of the L2 level) did not reach the performance level required to earn a decent living, though they remained in the network for a long time.

The MNC in IDN4 was the only case that provided a different picture. It used networks and the social capital of a global NGO to select and manage micro-sellers, without demanding women's full-time dedication or using paternalistic policies; rather it treated micro-sellers as customers. L2 micro-sellers kept more frequent contact with alternative distributors—who sold directly to some L2s—than with L1 micro-sellers. L1 micro-sellers receded as the model evolved, and alternative distributors preferred to sell directly to L2 micro-sellers to avoid commissions. L2 sellers did not compete in high-density areas, as they worked with alternative distributors. The size of the Brazilian market was large enough to avoid cannibalisation and conflicts with traditional channels. At the time of the evaluation, the retention rate was 75%, higher than the 3% to 10% of the other IDNs.

The effect of inertias on social value creation

These networks gave BOP women access to goods and services they could not autonomously acquire, therefore creating social value. These benefits included access to funding, training, and other incentives used by anchor organisations to reduce turnover. IDN1 offered microcredits and health insurance, in alliance with an NPO. Micro-sellers also received prizes tied to sales and participated in raffles. IDN3 offered a school savings plan, life insurance, and a health program. The company also implemented incentives for high-performing micro-sellers. However, many micro-sellers had no knowledge of or did not use these benefits.

Regarding credit programs, few micro-sellers knew of the availability of these programs and, as the model evolved, all those who used financing tools did so for purposes other than the intended. IDN1 included an NPO that offered microcredits, but during scale-up, the use of microcredits did not grow at the same pace as the channel's recruitment. This recruitment, initially facilitated by the NPO, was replaced by referrals. The social enterprise of IDN2 chose not to offer microcredits nor seek a financial ally to protect women from paying high interests or quitting the IDN while in debt. IDN3 facilitated access to the formal financial system (bancarisation) as an additional benefit, but micro-sellers saw it as just another rule with which they had to comply in order to become part of the IDN and to pay and receive payments. IDN4 did not require financing, as micro-sellers were used to paying with a credit card. IDN5 provided two weeks for payment but did not offer microcredits.

In general, regarding the effects of training programs, micro-sellers claimed that training provided valuable professional and personal life tools as well as the opportunity to put such tools into practice. Companies also developed more specific training programs that better responded to the sellers' needs. IDN4 had a 36-hour program on entrepreneurship, nutrition, and life, after which the micro-seller had to show sales skills in the field. IDN5 sought to optimise costs. Its training model had three stages: Mentoring, training workshops, and business management. The mentoring stage was dropped due to high cost, and training workshops were run by company directors to reduce cost. IDN1 formed a partnership with an NPO to train micro-sellers. IDN3 relied on a local bank and external consultants to provide specific training. However, some micro-sellers stated that they had no time to attend in-person training. In response, IDN4 added some virtual training for L2 micro-sellers.

Companies made generalised efforts to provide micro-entrepreneurs with direct support. IDN3, for example, had a support team (store representatives) who responded to micro-sellers' queries, clarified accounts, and retrained micro-sellers. IDN1 gave direct support to L1 micro-sellers and looked for ways to take training to their geographical areas. Participation in IDNs increased some micro-sellers' sense of belonging. They saw themselves as members of a big family, sharing life experiences, expectations, and struggles. IDN1 micro-sellers spoke about their role in a growing family, even as partners of the MNC. IDN3 micro-sellers showed the weakest sense of belonging, perceiving themselves as "just employees."

Strategies to reduce desertion—which had questionable results in practice—showed that, though companies believed incentives and gifts were appropriate, these did not tackle the real and specific causes of desertion, and micro-sellers did not see their aggregated value. Besides, reliable micro-sellers seemed to stay longer in the IDNs, mostly due to their personal traits, professional profiles, and tolerance to frustration, rather than as a result of said strategies.

The effect of inertias on interaction value creation

Changes to control distribution costs, route planning, and ICTs reinforced inertias and affected another dimension of the value proposition: Cross-sectoral value creation. By reducing "cross-sectorality," interaction value was diminished. Coordination constituted one of their most salient challenges for IND participants. At the time of the evaluation, team members of one of the IDNs did not know their counterparts. Another IDN reported weak and uncoordinated communication throughout the project's execution. Only IND4 showed a high level of institutionalisation of communication and coordination with partners.

Challenges in managing cross-sectoral coordination were related to internal barriers within the organisations, relationships between for-profit and nonprofit organisations, and communication difficulties. At the start-up phase, all projects admitted the need for cross-sector collaboration, which diminished during scale-up.

Executive officers within the organisations had different backgrounds and experience, which created diverse expectations around the IDN's final goal, raising internal barriers within the organisations. While some placed emphasis on profitability, others sought to reach the highest social impact through a self-sustainable model. One participant in IDN3 elaborated:

> When we started closing stores, people of the administrative team were so demotivated that they felt they have failed. I talked to each one of them, as I recognised it is difficult to deal with social and business focuses at the same time. They live and know the stories of each micro-seller; therefore they are emotionally involved.

Executives of IDN5's social enterprise considered that the IDN was not as profitable and efficient as their traditional channels. The manager, however, still believed in the project's social value. The closing of several IDN3 stores generated opposing views between operative employees and the administrative team. While operative employees regretted closing down the stores and weighed the social impact they had on micro-sellers' lives, the administrative team placed greater emphasis on the sustainability of the entire IDN, directing resources to stores that performed well and complied with the model's policies. IDN2 evolved to become an urban operation and serve TOP markets, leading to a concern of whether this model would adequately comply with the primary mandate of social impact in rural areas. Despite the NPO's wish to have social impact, it was clear that IDN2 did not follow a philanthropic model. If economic sustainability was not reached, IDN2 had to close. Even the MNC in IDN1 encountered initial resistance from managers. To attain greater acceptance and involvement, executives from the MNC worked for three days with IDN1 beneficiaries in their neighborhoods in an attempt to overcome those barriers.

Disagreements between partners were frequent and affected the relationships between for-profit and nonprofit organisations in the ecosystem. The MNC of IDN4 experienced organisational and coordination difficulties with the local NGO. While the MNC expected fast financial results, the NGO took its time in recruiting and training micro-sellers. They created a cross-organisational team to make decisions and to reconcile their disparate viewpoints. On the other hand, IDN1 was an example of successful coordination between the MNC and its partners, especially with the NPO. Both organisations took advantage of their differences to develop an integrated model, composed of technical teams highly involved with IDN1. The MNC understood that the NPO's social expertise was vital to the launching of IDN1.

Communication among different groups within the IDN was crucial. IDN2 and IDN3 revealed a disconnection between micro-sellers and top executives. Micro-sellers expressed their concerns about demand trends, commercial practices, and improvement opportunities for the business model. But these ideas were only seldom evaluated or executed. One of the reasons for developing an IDN was to draw from micro-sellers' social capital and direct contact with customers. Communication with partners was essential in attaining coordination between partners. IDN2 stood out for its ineffective communication among actors. There were nodes through which information flowed, but communication difficulties were frequent. Parties had no shared vision, nor did they report early alerts or supervision strategies. Information coordination, command, reporting, and document flows were not entirely clear.

As IDNs became more effective in the BOP markets, the need for cross-sector alliances diminished. In IDN4, distributors and the MNC itself learned how to recruit employees, gradually replacing the NGO in this role. For IDN1, the NPO lost relevance in the scale-up because recruitment and funding were internalised by the MNC. IDN5 presented tensions between the social enterprise's economic and social logic and the economic perspective of the partner beverage company. Expectations were not aligned: While the social enterprise expected the IDN to represent 10% of its sales, the local food and beverage company thought that 5% would be enough. They did not even agree on the composition of the product portfolio. In sum, cases that had an MNC or and NGO as their anchor organisation internalised most functions, whereas, cases in which social enterprises were anchor organisations maintained frequent tensions and disagreements around the matter of social and economic value creation, even to the point of going bankrupt. Interaction value was difficult to create either because of learning and internalisation or due to irreconcilable differences.

Inventory management and reinforced inertias

Anchor organisations sought to reduce inventory loss and default rates, which made inventory management more complex for NGOs and social enterprises that did not own production. IDN3 exemplifies this complexity. The NGO made weekly deliveries through sales representatives. L1 micro-sellers placed orders, received products on consignment, and paid back what was owed the following week. Representatives limited the number of products to be delivered. Meanwhile, some L1 micro-sellers ordered small amounts of products to prevent them from expiring or for fear of not selling them. Although small orders reduced inventory storage costs and risks, stores went frequently out of stock and had low sales levels. More critical still was the fact that only 125 types of products (SKUs) were made available, in comparison to traditional convenience stores, which offered more than 2000 SKUs. Another challenge was to manage a portfolio of exclusively healthy products, with high margins and rotation, when consumers and L1 micro-sellers demanded traditional products. For IDN3, rigid inventory management policies led to an unmet demand and to the loss of consumers' trust.

Consignment products were another inventory management challenge due to potential losses from damaged products and through supply coordination. In IDN2, L1 micro-sellers received products without collateral and returned goods that were no longer adequate for sale. The model later evolved toward cash payments only. In IDN3's NGO, products on consignment were left on a weekly basis, partial payment was required in advance, and the balance payable upon actual delivery. Shortages were more frequent than returns.

These changes in inventory management reinforced inertias in the distribution, such as privileging traditional products with high turnover and low prices. Micro-sellers shifted from healthy products to less-nutritive foods that were easier to sell.

The effect of inertias on social value for customers

The adjustments made to the product mix penalised inclusion and nutrition criteria. IDN1 micro-sellers were negatively affected by frequent changes in the portfolio composition, because customers looked for certain products that did not find consistently. The company in this IDN even faced strong criticism—through an article published by a well-known newspaper—for the incidence of obesity caused by the nutritional composition of its products. The product mix for IDN2 changed due to its suppliers' instability, low margins, and the unavailability of certain products in distributors' warehouses, which affected the relationship between micro-sellers and communities. One of the supervisors in this IDN affirmed:

Sometimes there was stock out. Customers ordered products that suppliers did not replenish, due to a lack of alliances with them. The IDN should have worked very well if the stock was there, as long as L2 micro-sellers had enough sales levels and L1 micro-sellers were reaching new customers and enjoying growing sales. After portfolio changed and we run out of stock, everything started to fall apart.

In IDN5, the social enterprise's product mix, combined with the beverages of its allied company, seemed to be a point of disagreement, because the social enterprise wanted to increase the proportion of its products (10% to 25% to an expected 50%). For IDN3, a portfolio of 125 products did not seem enough to secure the model's sustainability, in comparison to the 2000 products that regular stores have. The network went from 400 stores, in 2012, to just 39, with 14 of them selling about US $700. Micro-sellers often asked for a wider product offer, with more rotation and higher margins, but the NGO refused. In general, fresh products posed additional logistical challenges. Yet another challenge was to find the right balance between quality and price. While some customers preferred low prices, others remained loyal to brands. Cheaper products or small packages were not always preferred.

Only IDN4 sustained a healthy product portfolio with high availability and fair prices. Its MNC managed micro-sellers as customers and listened to their advice. Instead of considering micro-sellers as an instrument to launch new products or sell goods that could not be sold through other channels, the MNC conducted a market research and only sold products with high rotation. For all others, the tradeoff between social and economic value creation became evident as the initial value proposition of high quality, nutritional products changed. IDNs shifted to cheaper and less nutritional products with more affordable prices and higher turnover.

Financial sustainability and reinforced inertias

In relation to the IDNs' financial sustainability, we identified challenges in meeting a break-even point and achieving economies of scale. IDN processes of recruitment, training, support, retention, and monitoring were costly. All IDNs achieved break-even points in times longer than those expected by the anchor organisations. Models with anchor MNCs that owned production (IDN1 and IDN4) were more flexible than the multi-supplier models led by NGOs (IDN3) or social enterprises (IDN2 and IDN5). Anchor companies that owned production enjoyed financial flexibility due to other previously established distribution channels, appropriation and knowledge of design and production, and more control over production costs and margins. NGOs and social enterprises had to negotiate with powerful suppliers and reduce their margins to offer attractive margins for entrepreneurs, as illustrated in this testimony from one leader of IDN2:

> For inclusive distribution to work for fast moving consumer goods you need to include suppliers, a partnering, truly partnering, with a long-term outlook

[...] I do think that patient capital doesn't just mean putting money on the table, it means those suppliers truly partnering with a long-term outlook of what this distribution model means for those communities and those markets.

Investments in social capital delayed profitability, as anchors had to train micro-sellers to create and develop long-term relationships with customers. Companies had to make high initial investments and cover recurrent operational costs associated with increasing sales, while micro-sellers strengthened their social capital and increased their sales volume. When IDN1 met its break-even point, profitability was not as high as expected. The MNC determined that, instead of profit maximisation, it merely needed to cover costs, compensating the IDN channel with profits from other channels. The social value of the IDN was still highly valued and incorporated into the MNC's sustainability reports. IDN2, IDN3, and IDN5 had not met their break-even points by the time evaluations were conducted. IDN4 was growing at the pace of traditional channels and met its break-even point within the timeframe of the evaluation.

Economies of scale in IDNs have dynamics of their own. IDNs are labor-intensive and require high sales volumes to compensate the low profitability per unit, especially for mass consumption products. This poses a dilemma: The IDN needs to increase sales, which implies raising the number of micro-sellers and their productivity. When the distribution channel grows, however, operational costs also rise. Key variables to augment sales and profitability included: Training, empowerment, and micro-seller retention levels; ICTs for logistics (to ease trace-ability of inventories and routes, orders, control of chain of command and to increase the L2 to L1 micro-sellers' ratio); and balance between control and flex-ibility in the management of micro-sellers that allowed them to take proactive decisions when convenient for the business.

The dominant focus of IDNs in the scale-up phase was to achieve financial sustainability. This reinforced the search for economic efficiencies. The pressure to meet break-even points moved IDNs to scaled-up traditional business models. Anchor organisations reinforced the "business as usual" inertia, without any concern for the environmental impacts of the products and activities of the IDN.

The effect of inertias on environmental value

The IDNs start-up business models had a narrow view of sustainability, focusing exclusively on the economic and social aspects of the value proposition. The mass distribution of products packaged to serve the needs of the BOP population increased the amount of waste. In the case of IDN2, waste disposal ended up in very well-preserved sites in deep rural Peru, destroying their cultural and environmental value. In an estimation of the aggregated environmental impact of the five scaled-up IDNs, we found an increase of plastic waste of about 258 million units of single-use plastics per year. Also, IDNs distributing to remote areas increased the greenhouse emissions per box of products from 0.00027 tons of CO_2/month in their primary routes to about 0.0116 tons of CO_2/month per box in the tertiary routes where the IDN sold and delivered the products for the BOP segment.

All IDNs in the sample included a set of social components in their start-up business models: Presence of social organisations in their ecosystems; funds from cooperation agencies whose mandate was to promote sustainable development; and social value elements of inclusion and nutrition in their value propositions. All these elements either disappeared from the value propositions and organisational ecosystems or, when maintained, made the IDN struggle to become financially sustainable. In the scaled-up models, we found that, even though actions had affected all these elements, the anchor organisations rhetoric about the IDNs did not change. Furthermore, despite the changes and adjustments made to the scaled-up business models, the anchor organisations used IDN data to build their sustainability reports. As such, the IDNs' models continued to be legitimised as shared value or CSR models. This decoupling mechanism bolstered the sustainability "ceremony," regardless of the IDNs' diminished capacity to create social value and the destruction of environmental value in the BOP channel. All in all, we ended up with IDN business models that were legitimised as cross-sector business models for sustainability, but that, after the scale-up, were, in fact, neither cross-sector, nor sustainable.

Discussion: IDNs' potential and limitations

We show how IDNs, in their evolution toward achieving financial sustainability, strengthen the economic aspects of the value proposition, creating greater benefits for the MNCs. IDNs led by NGOs and social enterprises find it harder to meet a break-even point.

Throughout the scale-up process, however, the initial value proposition changes for all other stakeholders—micro-sellers, BOP consumers, and social organisations. Most micro-sellers experience an income increase while losing flexibility and autonomy through the IDN's process to scale up. The most significant benefits are captured by a reduced number of women (L1 micro-sellers with superior performance), with minimal benefits for women who strictly belong to the BOP. The effect is regressive because the increase in income for IDN women at the start comes at the expense of benefits to local micro-stores that served these markets before the IDN's existence. Consumers have access to an evolving, not necessarily better, portfolio of products. The role of social organisations became less important as the IDN evolved. IDNs destroy environmental value by increasing waste and emissions. Despite this evidence, IDN models continued to be legitimised as shared value models, and companies include them in their sustainability reports, illustrating the use of decoupling mechanisms to legitimise these projects.

Our contribution contradicts the positive bias of IDN research and has implications for theory and practice. We complement research on tradeoffs between social, environmental, and economic value creation through initiatives that address BOP needs. We contribute to previous research on alliances (Gutiérrez et al., 2016) by studying the evolution of alliance portfolios from a sample with heterogeneous portfolios and different legal modalities and by connecting configuration patterns with performance outcomes. We identify internal mechanisms, whereby anchor organisations in IDNs gain efficiencies to diminish the cross-sectorial aspect of the ecosystem.

The mechanisms used by MNCs to scale up IDNs are as follows: Adjustments to elements of the supply chain related to distribution costs, routing plans, and use of ICTs, as well as changes in inventory management and financial sustainability. Most of these adjustments are difficult to make when the anchor organisation is an NGO or a social enterprise. We identify and expose tradeoffs in the creation of social, economic, and environmental value for the diverse stakeholders involved in IDNs: Women, consumers, the organisational ecosystem, and the environment. When micro-sellers are rearranged into levels (i.e., pyramidal structure), they lose flexibility and autonomy. Women in the higher L1 levels capture most of the value, yet these women no longer belong to the vulnerable BOP population. Economic value capture in successfully scaled-up IDNs does not follow a progressive pattern, contributing to societal inequality. We show explicit and subtle mechanisms with which firms skew value distribution and capture, proposing an alternative explanation to research in this field (Bapuji et al., 2018).

We also used data-following implementation for a time span longer than that of previous studies (Reficco and Gutiérrez, 2016) to extend previous research. Our findings illustrate inertias in the distribution field that were reinforced by the changes in the business models: Maintaining the power and status of traditional distributors and firms' dependencies with these distributors; reinforcing social exclusion and last-mile constraints; privileging portfolios of non-nutritive high-turnover foods in the product mix; reducing flexibility for micro-sellers by imposing strict controls on their time and movements without formalising their labor; and concentrating control of the anchor organisations on the organisational ecosystem. Reinforcing these inertias constrain the possibility of organisations reaching ambidexterity when the BOP business model is focused on distribution. The whole distribution system is so highly institutionalised that exploiting inertia becomes too strong to resist and thus thwarts sustainability.

In our work, we overcome the limitations of previous studies in this field, yet we are also aware of our research limitations. The most salient of these is that a single case per country in our sample does not allow us to untangle the effect of the level of market development on IDN evolution or its prospects for success or failure during the scale-up. Our sample suggests that the high level of development of the Brazilian market played a role in the types of adaptations made by the BM and in the superior performance of IDN4. Further research could shed light on how this and other country-specific contextual and institutional variables affect the evolution of a BM and its prospects for success. Additional research is also needed to determine the effects of promoting a consumption culture in BOP women and how this affects other dimensions of their quality of life. Finally, we also identify and estimate the negative environmental impact of IDNs, but other studies could deepen on this specific outcome to provide more details on the mechanisms by which IDNs destroy this type of value.

The main implications for practice relate to understanding the difficulties and possibilities of creating inclusive business in the distribution. From the different organisational forms in our sample, MNCs were the more successful in this endeavor. The limited resources and capabilities of social enterprises and NGOs impose several constraints on a scaled-up IDN achieving financial sustainability in a field with powerful actors (traditional distributors) and a strong inertia-privileging economic efficiency. The comparison of MNCs in the sample also allowed us to see that the performance of IDN4 operating in the Brazilian market was very different from the other MNCs. We identified the reasons for the success of IDN4 as follows: The selection of the global NGO as a strategic partner; quality and availability of products; flexibility for micro-sellers; access to capital and credit card advances in the financial system for micro-sellers; and the structuring of an alternative distribution network with small and medium enterprises. The first three conditions were related to IDN management, while the last two portrayed a more developed market with fewer market failures (banking levels and not monopolised distribution). The combination of these factors allowed the company to reach positive results. These lessons can be learned by other organisations attempting to provide social, economic, and environmental value for BOP markets.

Appendix 1. Income pyramids

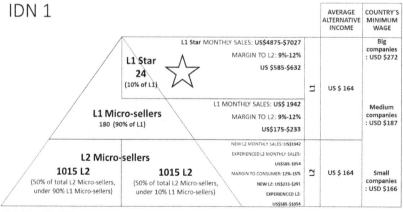

Data: December, 2016

IDN 2

		AVERAGE ALTERNATIVE INCOME	COUNTRY'S MINIMUM WAGE

L1 Micro-sellers

L1 MONTHLY SALES: US$150-$460
MARGIN TO L2: 5%
US $23-$115

L1 → US $ 100

L2 Micro-sellers

L2 MONTHLY SALES: US$120
MARGIN TO CONSUMER: 20% (US$24)

L2 → US $ 100

US $228

Data: December, 2015. 43 active L1 Micro-sellers, and approximately 700 active L2 Micro-sellers by December, 2015. 818 L1 and L2 Micro-sellers by June, 2018.

IDN 3

		AVERAGE ALTERNATIVE INCOME	COUNTRY'S MINIMUM WAGE

L1 TOP stores
(6,8% of 205) =14 stores

L1 MONTHLY SALES: US$700-$1330
MARGIN TO FINAL CONSUMER: 15%
US $105-$200

91 L1 Regular stores
Opened from September of 2016
38 stores (regular stores and TOP stores)
operating the first quarter of 2018

L1 REGULAR STORES MONTHLY SALES: US$220-$588
MARGIN TO FINAL CONSUMER: 15% (US$33-$88)

L1 → Less than US 175

US $175

Data: February, 2018. Minimum wage in the country is established by industrial sector. This presented wage is the average of all sectors, by February, 2018.

IDN 4

		AVERAGE ALTERNATIVE INCOME	COUNTRY'S MINIMUM WAGE

L1 Micro-sellers

L1 MONTHLY SALES: US$200-$800
MARGIN TO FINAL CONSUMER: 30%
US $60-$240
MARGIN TO L2: 3,5%
US $60-$240

L1 → US $ 60

L2 Micro-sellers

L2 MONTHLY SALES: US$200-$800
MARGIN TO CONSUMER: 30%
US$60-$240

L2 → US $ 60

US $231

Data: December, 2017. 2788 L1 and L2 Micro-sellers. This IDN had margin to final consumer because L1 Micro-sellers sold directly to consumers, besides sales to L2 Micro-sellers.

IDN 5

Data: December, 2016. 40 L1 Micro-sellers and 8 L2 Micro-sellers by June, 2018. This IDN had margin to final consumer because L1 Micro-sellers sold directly to consumers, besides sales to L2 Micro-sellers.

Note

1 We kept "NPO" as an organisation identifier when the organisation referred to itself as such. In an analogous manner, we kept "NGO" as an identifier for the organisation when it was identified as such.

References

Abdelkafi, N., & Tauscher, K. (2016). Business models for sustainability from a system dynamics perspective. *Organization and Environment*, 29, 74–96.

Bapuji, H., Husted, B.W., Lu, J., & Mir, R. (2018). Value creation, appropriation, and distribution: How firms contribute to societal economic inequality. *Business & Society*, 57, 983–1009.

Bendul, J., Rosca, E., & Pivovarova, D. (2017). Sustainable supply chain models for base of the pyramid. *Journal of Cleaner Production*, 16, 1–14.

Bocken, N.M.P., Rana, P., & Short, S.W. (2015). Value mapping for sustainable business thinking. *Journal of Industrial and Production Engineering*, 32, 67–81.

Bocken, N.M.P., Short, S.W., Rana, P., & Evans, S. (2014). A literature and practice review to develop sustainable business model archetypes. *Journal of Cleaner Production*, 65, 42–56.

Bosma, N., Acs, Z., Autio, E., Coduras, A., & Levie, J. (2009). *Global Entrepreneurship Monitor, 2008. Executive Report*. Babson Park, MA: Babson College; Santiago, Chile: Universidad del Desarollo. UK: Global Entrepreneurship Research Association.

Camenzuli, A., & McKague, K. (2015). Team microfranchising as a response to the entrepreneurial capacity problem in low-income markets. *Social Enterprise Journal*, 11, 69–88.

Chatnani, N. (2010). Women's empowerment through microfranchising. *Amity Global Business Review*, 5, 24–37.

Chelekis, J., & Mudambi, S.M. (2010). MNCs and micro-entrepreneurship in emerging economies: The case of Avon in the Amazon. *Journal of International Management*, 16, 412–424.

Chikweche, T., & Fletcher, R. (2011). Franchising at the Bottom of the Pyramid BOP: An alternative distribution approach. *The International Review of Retail, Distribution and Consumer Research*, 21, 343–360.

Christensen, L., Lehr, D., & Fairbourne, J (2010a) A good business for poor people. *Stanford Social Innovation Review*, 8, 44–49.

Crane, A., Palazzo, G., Spence, L.J., & Matten, D. (2014). Contesting the value of "creating shared value". *California Management Review*, 60, 130–146.

Daley, J. (2014). It takes a village. *Entrepreneur Magazine*, April, 92–99.

Dembek, K., York, J., & Singh, P. J (2018). Creating value for multiple stakeholders: Sustainable business models at the Base of the Pyramid. *Journal of Cleaner Production*, 196, 1600–1612.

Dolan, C. (2012). The new face of development: The 'bottom of the pyramid' entrepreneurs. *Anthropology Today*, 28, 3–7.

Dolan, C., Johnstone, L., & Scott, L. (2012). Shampoo saris and SIM cards seeking entrepreneurial futures at the bottom of the pyramid. *Gender and Development*, 20, 33–47.

Esko, S., Zeromskis, M., & Hsuan, J. (2013) Value chain and innovation at the base of the pyramid. *South Asian Journal of Global Business Research*, 2, 230–250.

Gimenez, C., Sierra, V., & Rodon, J. (2012). Sustainable operations: Their impact on the triple bottom line. *International Journal of Production Economics*, 140, 149–159.

Gold, S., Hahn, R., & Seuring, S. (2013) Sustainable supply chain management in "Base of the Pyramid" food projects—A path to triple bottom line approaches for multinationals? *International Business Review*, 22, 784–799.

Gutiérrez, R., Márquez, P., & Reficco, E. (2016). Configuration and development of alliance portfolios: A comparison of same-sector and cross-sector partnerships. *Journal of Business Ethics*, 135, 55–69.

Hahn, R. (2009). The ethical rational of business for the poor—Integrating the concepts Bottom of the Pyramid, sustainable development, and corporate citizenship. *Journal of Business Ethics*, 84, 313–324.

Hahn, R., & Gold, S. (2014). Resources and governance in "base of the pyramid"-partnerships. *Journal of Business Research*, 67, 1321–1333.

Hill, S.A., & Birkinshaw, J. (2012). Ambidexterity and survival in corporate venture units. *Journal of Management*, 40, 1899–1931.

Jones, L. (2008). Alleviating poverty using microfranchising models: Case studies and a critique. In Wankel, C. (Eds.), *Alleviating Poverty Through Business Strategy* (pp. 149–170). New York: Palgrave Macmillan.

Kandachar, P., & Halme, M. (2007). Introduction. *Greener Management International*, 51, 3–17.

Kistruck, G., Webb, J., & Sutter, C. (2011) Microfranchising in base of the pyramid. *Entrepreneurship: Theory and Practice*, 35, 503–531.

Mair, J., & Marti, I. (2012). Building inclusive markets in rural Bangladesh: How intermediaries work institutional voids. *Academy of Management Journal*, 55, 819–850.

Meyer, J.W., & Rowan, B (1977). Institutionalized organizations: Formal structure as myth and ceremony. *American Journal of Sociology*, 83, 340–363.

Norton, S.W. (1988). Franchising, brand name capital, and the entrepreneurial capacity problem. *Strategic Management Journal*, 9, 105–114.

Prahalad, C.K. (2005). *The Fortune at the Bottom of the Pyramid: Eradicating Poverty Through Profits*. New Delhi: Wharton School Publishing.

Pullman, M.E., Maloni, M.J., & Carter, C.R. (2009). Food for thought: Social versus environmental sustainability practices and performance outcomes. *Journal of Supply Chain Management*, 45, 38–54.

Reficco, E., & Gutiérrez, R. (2016). Organizational ambidexterity and the elusive quest for successful implementation of BOP ventures. *Organization & Environment*, 29, 461–481.

Rivera-Santos, M., & Rufin, C. (2010). Global village vs. small town: Understanding networks at the Base of the Pyramid. *International Business Review*, 19, 126–139.

Smith, N.C. (2008). Consumers as drivers of corporate social responsibility. In A. Crane, D. Matten, A. McWilliams, & D.S. Siegel (Eds.), *The Oxford Handbook of Corporate Social Responsibility* (pp. 281–302). Oxford: Oxford University Press.

Sodhi, M., & Tang, C. (2013). Supply chain research opportunities with the poor as suppliers or distributors in developing countries. *Production and Operations Management*, 23, 1483–1494.

Stubbs, W., & Cocklin, C. (2008). Conceptualizing a "Sustainability business model." *Organization and Environment*, 21, 103–127.

Vachani, S., & Smith, C. (2008). Socially responsible distribution. distribution strategies for reaching the Bottom of the Pyramid. *California Management Review*, 50, 52–84.

Van Kirk, G. (2010) The microconsignment model: Bridging the "Last Mile" of access to products and services for the rural poor. *MIT Journal Innovation*, 5, 101–127.

Viswanathan, M., & Sridharan, S. (2009). From subsistence marketplaces to sustainable marketplaces: A bottom-up perspective of the role of business in poverty alleviation. *Ivey Business Journal*, March-April.

Wankel, C. (2008). *Alleviating Poverty Through Business Strategy*. New York: Palgrave Macmillan.

Webb, J.W., Kistruck, G.M., Ireland, R.D., & Ketchen, D.J. Jr (2010). The entrepreneurship process in base of the pyramid markets: The case of multinational enterprise/nongovernment organisation alliances. *Entrepreneurship: Theory and Practice*, 34, 555–581.

Whiteman, G., & Cooper, W. (2016). Decoupling rape. *Academy of Management Discoveries*, 2, 115–154.

Yang, M., Evans, S., Vladimirova, D., & Rana, P. (2017). Value uncaptured perspective for sustainable business model innovation. *Journal of Cleaner Production*, 140, 1784–1804.

Index

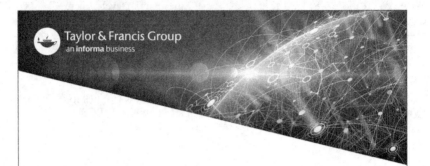

Printed in the United States
by Baker & Taylor Publisher Services